The Chalukyas of Badami

The Chalukyas of Badami

Edited by
S. Rajasekhara

INTACH
Aryan Books International

THE CHALUKYAS OF BADAMI

ISBN: 978-81-7305-553-9

Published in **2016** by

INTACH

The Indian National Trust for Art and Cultural Heritage
71, Lodhi Estate, New Delhi - 110003

and

Aryan Books International

Pooja Apartments, 4B, Ansari Road, New Delhi-110 002 (India)
Tel.: 23287589, 23255799; Fax: 91-11-23270385
E-mail: aryanbooks@gmail.com
www.aryanbooks.co.in

Designed and Printed in India by
ABI Prints & Publishing Co., New Delhi

Contents

Preface

The Dharwad Chapter of INTACH had the good fortune of hosting a two-day National Seminar in May 2011 on the cultural contribution made by the Chalukyan Kings of Badami.

The eminent historian Prof. (Dr.) S. Rajasekhara had kindly consented to be the Director of this seminar. Eminent scholars and historians from different parts of India participated in the seminar and presented their papers.

The Badami Chalukyas (*c.* AD 535–AD 757) ruled over a large territory in India. One of their kings, Pulakesi II defeated Harshavardhana of Kanauj on the banks of the river Narmada and became justly famous on that account.

The Chalukyas of Badami played a pivotal role in the history and culture of the Deccan, nay, of India itself. The Chalukyan kings of Badami were successors to the Kadambas of Banavasi (who laid the foundation of the Karnataka empire). The Chalukyan kings of Badami, by dint of military power, expanded it and built a vast empire form Narmada down to Kaveri and from Western ocean to the Eastern.

They thus built up a unified Karnataka as it were, bringing under its umbrella smaller powers that had spread over the entire land. They coined the name Karnataka to this empire. Their army came to be reckoned as invincible 'Karnataka Bala'.

The Chalukyan kings of Badami sponsored all religions of the land irrespective of their personal affiliations. They were trend-setters in the field of architecture, which is vouchsafed by astounding monuments, caves as well as structures.

It is well known that Pattadakal, their sub-capital, was known for its temples. Aihole, another Chalukyan art centre, is often referred to as the 'cradle of Indian architecture'. The flourishing trade and commerce built up a strong economy. The Kannada language got, for the first time, the official status and came to be employed liberally in the inscriptions, which were the mouth-pieces of the rulers and their administrative subordinates. Thus, covering a period of over 200 years and more, the Chalukyan period formed a fundamental epoch in the history and culture of our land.

Among the various relics left by the Chalukyan kings, reference must be made to Pattadakal, which is today considered as a 'World Heritage Site'. Visitors from far and near will find these historical relics dating back to Badami Chalukyan times as richly rewarded, as they are truly unrivalled and majestic in their grandeur. Hence, the saga of Badami Chalukyan kings is truly found to be a testimony to the splendour and glory of ancient India.

Many years ago, the Mythic Society in Bangalore had conducted a seminar on Badami Chalukyan kings and published a book based on the papers presented by scholars and historians.

The national seminar organized by INTACH, Dharwad was an attempt to revisit the history of Badami Chalukyan kings with a view to re-examine the contributions in the light of new material and evidences that have been found after Mythic Society's seminar. Hence, the readers will find this book highly informative as it throws new light on some of the hitherto unexplored areas of our culture and society. It is also assumed that the new material accumulated during this period would fulfil the need for bridging the gap and would strengthen the study of the subject. In addition, it would serve the purpose of acquiring and educating the new generation of scholars and enthuse them to carry on with their work in the light of earlier studies.

It gives me great pleasure in remembering all those who made it possible for INTACH, Dharwad Chapter to organize this seminar.

My sincere and deep debt of gratitude is to Prof. (Dr.) S. Rajasekhara, who has painstakingly helped our Chapter in planning and organizing this national seminar, which turned out to be a grand success. But for his devotion, missionary zeal and hard work, this seminar would have not taken place. He has also edited this book with his matchless scholarship, experience and know-how. The book is what it is because of his labour of love.

I am also beholden to all the eminent scholars and historians who responded to our request and came to Dharwad to present their scholarly papers.

I am grateful to Shri Jagadeesh Shettar, the then minister of the Karnataka Government who inaugurated this National Seminar.

I am also deeply obliged to Maj. Gen. (Retd.) L.K. Gupta, Chairman, INTACH, Delhi, who made it convenient to attend this seminar and who obliged us by granting munificent funds. He truly is an enlightened patriarch of INTACH extending his helping hand to all noble causes. I am also grateful to him for getting this book published.

I am also beholden to Shri. P.C. Naik, IAS (Retd.), former State Convenor, INTACH, who goaded me to organize this two-day seminar on Chalukyan kings of Badami. He has been a friend, philosopher and guide to our Chapter.

I must place on record my appreciation and gratitude to all the members of our Chapter, who gave me their unstinted cooperation in organizing this seminar.

I am beholden to my wife Dr. Yashoda Bhat (who is also a member of INTACH, Dharwad) for all the support and help extended to me in organizing this seminar.

N.P. Bhat
Convenor
Dharwad Chapter of INTACH
Dharwad

Editor's Note

The interest in early Chalukya studies, particularly art and architecture, more or less started with the publication of Jas Burgess' *Report of the First Season's Operations in the Belgaum and Kaladgi Districts (Jan-May 1874)*, wherein some account of early Chalukya monuments was attempted. However, it was the publication of Henry Cousens' *The Chalukyan Architecture of the Kanarese Districts* published in 1926 that really opened up the Chalukyan—both early and later—temples for a proper analysis. Cousens' work includes a description of the temples in the Kannada-speaking discricts of the erstwhile Bombay Presidency before India became independent. He tried to analyse the stylistic aspects and worked on a tentative chronology for the monuments. For long, till the sixties in the 20th century, Cousens' work was considered as the most reliable study and was quite often quoted by the scholars. Within three years of Cousens' publication, the Archaeological Survey of India published an excellent memoir titled *Bas Reliefs of Badami* written by R.D. Banerji. From the middle of the 20th century, a number of scholars like K.V. Soundararajan, K.R. Srinivasan, R.S. Gupte, D.P. Dikshit,

K.V. Ramesh, Gary Tarr, George Michell, S. Rajasekhara and Carol Radcliff, to name a few, undertook studies on different aspects of early Chalukya temples.

The foundation of the early Chalukya rule in the first half of the 6th century and its gradual expansion up to river Narmada resulted in political and economic stability, which had a great impact on temple constructional activities. The rulers were great supporters of Vedic culture. The construction of an impregnable fortress at Vatapi by Pulakesi I provided impetus for starting architectural activities. For building temples, the early Chalukyas selected those sites which were already sanctified in the local legends, traditions and puranas. The result was the emergence of Aihole, Mahakuta, Badami and Pattadakal in Karnataka and Alampur in Andhra Pradesh as great centres of art. There were other centres of Chalukya art like Naganathakolla, Siddhanakolla, Bhadra Nayakana Jalihal, Huligemmanakolla, Sulebhavi, Ittagi and Nargund in Karnataka and Kadamarakalava, Panyam, Papanasanam, Mahanandi, Satyavolu and Kudaveli Sangama (now submerged) in Andhra Pradesh. A study of the early Chalukya temples built in both Karnataka and Andhra Pradesh is useful to understand the development of architecture in these areas and also to assess the contribution of the early Chalukyas to South Indian art and architecture.

The early Chalukya period witnessed the introduction of a number of new aspects connected with art and architecture for the first time in the Deccan and the South. At Aihole, Mahakuta and Pattadakal, they introduced temples built in different styles of architecture—*Dravida, Rekha Nagara, Kadamba Nagara, Vesara*— in addition to temples with flat roofs, which are often referred to as *Mantapa* style of temples. This phenomenon was a significant feature of the Chalukya rule because in no other place do we come across the construction of temples in different styles side by side. What is amazing is that at Aihole they built temples on different plans. They built both *sandhara* and *nirandhara* temples. E.g., Huchchimalligudi, Durga, Melgudi are *sandhara* temples while Huchchappayyagudi, Tarappagudi, Mallikarjuna, Galaganatha and others temples are *nirandhara* temples. They also built temples on apsidal plan. The Durga is apsidal in shape. What is interesting is that it has two *pradakshinas*—one closed which is around the sanctum and the other which is half open around the inner *pradakshina, sabhamantapa* and the porch. The Gaudargudi (in reality Durga Bhagavati temple) has an open *pradakshina* located in the square pillared hall wherein the sanctum is built in the centre of the hall. Outside the Ravanaphadi cave is a small *Dravida* temple, which is one of the earliest *Dravida* temples of South India.

The Melgudi built in AD 634-35 is a landmark *basadi* as far as Jaina architecture is concerned. It has an upper sanctum built above the lower main sanctum. Its construction looks like an afterthought built a few years later. However, Melgudi provided the first example of a storeyed *basadi.* The Melgudi became a model to be emulated when it came to building storeyed *basadis.* The Jains in Karnataka were fascinated by the Melgudi and they continued this tradition of storeyed *basadis.* In the post early Chalukya period, such storeyed *basadis* were built during the period of the succeeding dynasties in Karnataka. As examples can be noted the Settavva temple at Aihole, the Jaina Narayana temple at Pattadakal, the Chavundaraya Basadi at Sravana Belgola and the Brahma Jinalaya at Lakkundi. In all these cases, the upper sanctum was built into the *sikhara* of the *basadi.*

Of late, a view has emerged that the Durga temple at Aihole originally did not possess a *rekha nagara sikhara* and that it was added subsequently at a later date from the debris of another temple. They think that a *rekha nagara sikhara* does not synchronize with an apsidal sanctum. This is contestable. When we look at the small apsidal temple at Hale Mahakuta, we find a few elements of the *rekha nagara sikhara* intact above the sanctum while the rest of the portion of the *sikhara* is lying nearby. It may be noted that this debris of the *rekha nagara sikhara* does not belong to any other structure in the vicinity. Near this apsidal temple are two temples of the Rahtrakuta and Later Chalukya periods. The main temple here possesses a *kadamba nagara sikhara.*

The Jambulinga temple at Badami, built in AD 699 by Vinayavati, mother of King Vijayaditya, is the first *trikuta* temple of the structural variety to be built in South India. This temple with three sanctums, which open into a large pillared hall with a porch outside the hall, had a great impact on the construction of temples in Karnataka. It inspired the construction of a huge number of *trikutas* in the post early Chalukya period under the Rashtrakutas, Kalyana Chalukyas and the Hoysalas. For example, at Aihole itself a few *trikutas* were built during the Rashtrakuta period.

The early Chalukya period witnessed the standardisation of iconographical features of Hindu deities and this standardisation was followed in the subsequent periods. For example, the sculpture of Varaha in Cave II at Badami shows Bhudevi standing on a lotus, which is placed in the lower left palm of Varaha and the goddess has placed her right hand on the snout of Varaha. In Cave III of the same place, Bhudevi stands on the palm of the lower left hand, which is raised. Here the goddess places her right hand on the left shoulder of Varaha, who is seen looking at her. The Varaha sculpture in the Ravanaphadi cave at Aihole shows Bhudevi sitting on the left shoulder of Varaha with her legs hanging down. It is this standardised form of Varaha that was followed in the post early Chalukya times.

During the early Chalukya period, a number of new aspects of art and architecture were introduced in the South. Some of these were already an integral part of the earlier Buddhist art. The credit for introducing narrative sculptures goes to the early Chalukyas. These were introduced first in the cave temples and later in the structural temples. In the caves at Badami, the beams were beautified with small reliefs depicting incidents from the *puranas* and the epics. In the structural temples like Virupaksha and Mallikarjuna, the narrative sculptures connected with the *Mahabharata, Ramayana, Yasodharacharita, Gangavatarana*, etc. were carved on the pillars. In the Papanatha temple at Pattadakal, the *Ramayana* panels were carved on the exterior of the walls. They were also carved in some instances on the basement of the temples as in the Mahakutesvara temple at Mahakuta. In course of time, narrative sculptures became popular particularly under the Hoysalas—as can be seen in the Hoysala temples at Halebid,

Basral, Javagal, Nuggihalli, Amritapur, Somanathapura and other places. Even under the Vijayanagara rule, the narrative sculpture continued to attract the attention of the sculptors. The temples at Tadapatri, Lepakshi, Penugonda, Hampi and Srisaila can be cited as examples for this.

The bracket figures which were introduced by the Buddhists in the form of *Salabhanjikas* inspired the early Chalukya artists. For the first time in Karnataka they were introduced in the caves at Badami. For example, in Cave 3 the façade pillars have these bracket figures representing Siva-Parvati, Rati-Manmatha and other deities and *Nayikas*. There are as many as 32 bracket figures in this cave. The Chalukyas of Kalyana, Hoysalas and the Kakatiyas continued the tradition of accommodating bracket figures in their temples.

The credit for popularising the Siva-Nataraja sculptures in the Deccan goes to the early Chalukyas. The oldest Nataraja sculpture in South India is the one carved just outside Cave I at Badami. This eighteen-armed Nataraja in *chatura* pose has been the subject of many discussions. Nataraja here is beautiful, graceful and is unrivalled by any other Nataraja sculpture in the South. It is no wonder that this multi-armed Nataraja became an inspiration for the ten-armed Nataraja in the Ravanaphadi cave at Aihole. Many of the early Chalukya temples possess Nataraja sculptures either on the walls or in the *mahanasika* of the *rekha nagara sikhara*.

A very significant event which had great impact on early Chalukya art was the initiation of Vikramaditya I into *Sivamandala Dikshe*. Till then the early Chalukya rulers were devotees of Vaishnavism. But with the conversion of Vikramaditya I to Saivism, the early Chalukya rulers became staunch supporters of Saivism. More and more temples for Siva were built between AD 655 and AD 757. During this period, there was a considerable increase in the number of followers of Lakulisa. By the middle of the 6th century AD, Lakula Saivism was already taking deep roots in the early Chalukya Kingdom. A pillar sculpture in Cave I at Badami portrays the figures of Lakulisa and his four followers Kausika, Mitra, Garga and Kaurasya. Mahakuta emerged as a stronghold of the Lakula Saivas as testified by a number of sculptures of Lakulisa holding a staff on the walls and pillars of the temples at Mahakuta.

The early Chalukya period also witnessed the carving of some of the earliest sculptures of Bahubali and Parsvanatha. They are found on the walls of the Meena Basadi at Aihole and Cave IV at Badami. It is in these sculptures of Bahubali we find the crystallisation of the main iconographical features of Bahubali. Though inscriptions of the early Kadambas speak of Jain *basadis* and in fact a *basadi* for Bahubali called Kama Jinalaya, we are yet to find their remains. Under the early Chalukyas, the main features connected with Bahubali like *kayotsarga* posture, the ant-hills with snakes on either side of Bahubali, the entwining of creepers on the legs and arms of Bahubali were more or less standardised. However, in these sculptures Bahubali is shown with long hair falling up to the shoulders. It was during the time of the Rashtrakutas that the long hair was replaced by curly hair. In the Melgudi at Hallur, probably built during the time of Amoghavarsha I, we find on the outer walls sculptures of Bahubali in both the forms—with long hair as well as curly hair.

The early Chalukya temples basically contain square-shaped pillars. The façade pillars of Caves II and IV are unique because these pillars stand on the backs of lions, which are carved at the base. These could well be termed *vyaghrapada* pillars. Narasimhavarma I, the Pallava king who occupied Vatapi in AD 642, was impressed by this type of pillars. When he returned to his kingdom, he introduced them in his temples at Mahabalipuram with much more elaboration. The shaft in these pillars sits on the head of a lion, which is at the base of the pillar.

The present work is a collection of papers presented in a seminar on early Chalukyas of Badami organised by the Dharwad Chapter of Indian National Trust for Art and Cultural Heritage (INTACH) on 1st and 2nd April 2011 at Dharwad. The papers deal with different aspects of early Chalukya rule, their contribution to art and architecture, and the promotion of Chalukyan art centres as tourist destinations. Dr. A. Sundara has dealt with the prehistoric significance of the Badami area with special reference to rock-paintings. Dr. S.V. Padigar examines the name, origin and history of the early Chalukyas. The editor's paper examines in some details the important temples of the period—both rock-cut and structural—including their probable date of construction. The temples of Mahakuta and the legends connected with the place are dealt with by Dr. Meena Mohite. Dr. Sheelakant Pattar has tried to analyse the sculptural art of the early Chalukyas. Dr. K. Suryanarayana has attempted to focus attention on the early Chalukya rule in Andhradesa. Dr. Hampa Nagarajaiah writes on the Jaina aspects of the period. The paper by Mrs. Vandana Palankar deals with the promotion of Aihole-Pattadakal-Badami as tourist destinations. She examines the drawbacks in the promotion of these destinations. She also suggests steps to be taken to promote tourism in this part of north Karnataka. Shri V.M. Hegde writes on the urban planning of the early Chalukya towns. I take this opportunity to thank all these scholars for contributing their papers for publication.

S. Rajasekhara

Contributors

Dr. A. Sundara
Karikeya, Sharada Nagar, Sringeri - 577 139

Dr. S.V. Padigar
Mukunda, H.No. 60, 12th A Cross, Rani Chennammanagar, Dharwad - 580 001

Dr. Kolluru Suryanarayana
Dept. of History, Andhra University, Waltair (A.P.)

Dr. Nagarajaiah, Hampa (Hampana)
1079, 18th A Main, V Block, Rajajinagar, Bengaluru - 560 010

Dr. S. Rajasekhara
Saurabha, H.N. 11, 14th Cross, Rani Chennammanagar, Dharwad - 580 001

Dr. Sheelakant Pattar
Ishwarashilpa, Vidyanagar, Badami - 587 201

Dr. Meena M. Mohite
Dept. of History and Archaeology, Bhourao Kakatkar College Camp, Club Road, Belgaum

Mrs. Vandana Palankar
c/o S.A. Revankar, B/20, Vidyanagar,
Davanagere - 577 005

Shri V.M. Hegde
CEO, Centre for Symbiosis of Technology, Environment and Management (STEM), Bengaluru

1

Keynote Address
Understanding Our Great Cultural Heritage: Some Thoughts

A. Sundara

It is too well known that India has a very long and uninterrupted history and culture over a period of at least 5000 years. If prehistory of the land is taken into account, the antiquity of the cultural development through the ages goes back by several lakhs of years. The recently excavated archaeological material evidences of the earliest human cultural stage known as the Early Palaeolithic particularly from Hunasgi-Isampur (Surpur taluk, Gulbarga district, Karnataka) and Attirampakkam (near Chennai, Tamil Nadu), dated by scientific techniques, are respectively found to be about 10 and 15 lakh year old. Hundreds of prehistoric sites ranging from the earliest stage of the Old Stone Age (Palaeolithic) to the beginning of the historical era have been found all over the country. Studies of the explored and excavated materials have provided us a fairly good outline of our ancestors' cultural progress slowly but with acceleration from the remotest past. Broadly, seven developmental stages have been clearly vindicated in the cultural progress:

1-3. The early, middle, and upper Palaeolithic together known generally as the Old Stone Age or Palaeolithic.

4. Mesolithic indicating a transition from the nomadic food gathering to a rather settled lifestyle characterised by construction of dwellings, domestication of some categories of animals, such as sheep, goat, etc., governed by certain conventional traditions particularly with regard to the disposal of the dead.

5-6. Semi-urbanised Neolithic and Chalcolithic/Bronze Age settlements managed by chieftaincy

7. The Iron Age characterised by territorial control, advanced iron technology on large scale, putting an end to manufacturing of stone tools.

A very significant development from the upper Palaeolithic is rock art of three categories: cave painting, engraving and bruising on the bare rock surface. More than 5000 rock art sites are known so far from our country of which the Bhimbetka near Bhopal, Madhya Pradesh, is very well known, now inscribed as a World Heritage Site. Similarly, Hire Benkal-Hampi (Karnataka) area is profusely rich with such rock art, mostly cave paintings. The rock engravings in Edakal (Kerala) cave are unique, now fairly well known. Both the sites deserve to be inscribed as World Heritage Sites.

The Chalcolithic Sindhu-Saraswati Civilisation (*c.* 2500–1500 BCE) is phenomenal and is distinguished by its town-planning unknown in the other contemporary civilizations, such as the Mesopotamian, the Egyptian, etc., and its vast extent from Jammu to Surat and from Sukte Jendor near the western border of Pakistan to Atranjikhera in India comprising more than 2000 Harappa towns and rural settlements.

The last stage—the Iron Age—paved the way for the foundation of political nuclei and writing system for communication.

From the emergence of the 16 Maha Janapadas around 6th century BCE immediately followed by the most powerful and extensive Mauryan empire extending from Gandhara to the present-day north Karnataka region practically illustrating the ancient concept of *Chakravarti kshetram* of the ancient political thinkers and the Sangam society in the deep south, our great land witnessed intermittently the rise and fall of numerous kingdoms and dynasties, great and small, indigenous and alien up to the recent times. Whatever may be the merits and demerits, ideals and practices of the ruling dynasties of all stature, each one of them as well as some distinguished individuals did contribute something special in the field of art and architecture, literature, performing arts, science and technology, philosophy, etc. As a result, the whole country is adorned with works of great art. The simple but stately Mauryan pillars, the Mehrauli iron pillar, the historical Ajanta cave paintings, the colossal Gommateshvara in Sravana Belgola, the monolithic Kailash temple in Ellora, the Brihadishvara temple in Thanjavur, the Sun temple in Konark, the Jaina temples in Mount Abu, the Gol Gumbaz in Bijapur, the imposing Portuguese churches in old Goa, the Vijayanagar medieval city and its counterpart Fatehpur Sikri, in the north, etc. are but a few examples. Great thinkers such as philosophers, mathematicians, astronomers, polity and medicine, architecture and aesthetics brilliantly made the history of our country the most absorbing.

The foreigners visiting India from the beginning of the Western colonisation in India, on seeing such magnificent monuments especially and going through invaluable literature of our country, were simply wonderstruck about the amazingly great achievements of the Indian people. They began to write richly illustrated books about the architectural grandiose, philosophy and religion targeting the Western world. Consequently, there was an increasing flow of visitors to India just to see the Indian heritage and enjoy. Meanwhile, study and research on a very large scale was providing new insights for understanding our cultural heritage. Likewise, our people too being enlightened through various media are visiting these historical places. To meet the demands of various kinds and to provide facilities to them, the Departments of Tourism, State and Central, have been striving hard in various ways.

But the very nucleus of all these efforts is our heritage. Historians and history students are well aware of all these from the beginning to the recent. Though people at large, domestic and more so foreign, may know this brilliant story, but the knowledge is either very elementary or nil. They are to be provided therefore with educating information that makes them appreciate and enjoy the sightseeing and understand the Indian cultural spirit. No doubt, brief literature, guidebooks, maps, etc. are being prepared fairly well for them. But historical accounts with some examples would not really make people satisfied. It is just something what they came to know about them. Really speaking, the inside glory has to be revealed to them. Well, how do we understand our cultural heritage and present them in a way that they really feel proud, inspired and even provoked to do something good to the society like their ancestors? The main aim of this seminar is therefore to achieve this goal with a case study: The early Chalukya for the participants who in course of time will be ambassadors of our heritage in the world wherever they may be. Let me try to present in the way I visualize the early Chalukyan cultural heritage one by one.

1. As known from history, frequent wars meeting with success or failure, expansion or contraction of kingdoms so on and so forth are but common. In such critical situations, how the victor or the defeated would feel and behave in a magnanimous way is worthy of note. There are two instances in the history of the Chalukyas that need to be remembered. It is well known that Vikramaditya II conquered the Pallavas of Kanchi thrice; he then visited the Royal temple of Rajasimheshvara in Kanchi, which possessed enormous wealth. As a victor, he could have acquired all the wealth. But he didn't. Instead, he returned all the wealth to the temple with strict instructions that all religious activities should be carried on as before which is a rare example of magnanimity on the part of a victor. There is a Kannada inscription to this effect on one of the pillars of the temple. The main part of the text runs thus:

   Rājasiṁghēśvara dhanamān-kaṇḍu magaḷḍu dēvargge biṭṭar

The Kappe Arabhatta inscription in Badami begins with a *samskrita* verse:

varaṁtējasvino na tu manāvakhaṁḍanam /
mṛyus-tat-kṣṇikō duḥkham - mānabhaṁgaṁ dine dine //

What I have noticed in Badami is that this verse is engraved at two other places as well. Why is it repeatedly carved on stone? Palaeographically, the inscriptions may be dated to late 7th or early 8th century. Repeated engravings seem to indicate the deep pain that people experienced at the fall of their great hero Pulakesi II and Badami when Pallava Narisimhavarma I successfully invaded the capital. The piognant feelings expressed in the verse are simply heart-rending. Expressing deep concern for their country or kingdom and their ruler is a great virtue on the part of the people that may be comprehended here in this context. This is not an exceptional instance. Hundreds of *viragals* often carry a *samskrita* verse:

> *Jitēnāpi labhate Lakshmī mṛitenāpi surāṁganā /*
> *kṣaṇe vidhvamsinī kāye kā ciṁtā maraṇe raṇe //*

This is the most inspiring spirit of a true warrior fighting for a great and good cause.

2. The people in ancient Karnataka were great empire builders unparalleled in the history of South India. Pulakesi II expanded the kingdom with Narmada in the north, Kaveri in the south and the eastern and the western seas as the borders. Similarly, the Rashtrakuta and the Vijayanagar kingdoms were very vast. Neither the Pallava nor the Chola, nor the Pandya or the Adil Shahis were able to expand their kingdoms so extensively.
3. In the field of art and architecture, patrons, architects and sculptors stand highly distinguished. Since the kingdom was so vast including central India and the lower Deccan, naturally in addition to the regional architects, others from other parts also had participated in the programme of temple-building activity. Consequently, two main architectural forms: the *vimana,* i.e. Dravidian and the *Rekha Nagara,* i.e. Indo-Aryan, were adopted in Badami, Pattadakal and Aihole. To me it appears that the *vimana* form of architecture was developed by the Chalukyan architects of the early phase. This became in course of time very popular throughout South India. If my inference is correct, this is a great

contribution to the tradition of temple architecture by the Chalukyan architects. With regard to the *Rekha Nagara* form, of course, its incipient form could be seen in some Gupta temples that was perhaps refined by the Chalukyan architects. The very architect, Narasobba by name, of a temple of *Rekha Nagara* form in Aihole locally known as Huchchappayagudi proudly claims: ... *Jambū dvîpaaṁtare kaśchid vaastu prasaada tadgataḥ Narasobbasamō vidvān na bhūto nā bhavishyati.*

There is one more noteworthy point with regard to the development of temple architecture under the patronage of the ruling dynasty. The Chalukyan architects were innovative. In the Virupaksha and the Mallikarjuna temples, a successful attempt has been made to integrate a northern architectural component, namely *sukanasa* into the *vimana* architectural form. This particular resultant architectural form is often known as *vesara,* i.e. *misra* (mixed). This was in course of time very well developed and refined and became one of the most popular temple types during the Kalyana Chalukyan period. Henry Cousens designates this particular form as Chalukyan.

This is not all. The architects of the temples were greatly honoured by the kings. Again, Vikramaditya II comes to the scene in this regard. The architects of the two temples, now known as Virupaksha and Mallikarjuna but originally known as Lokeshvara and Trilokeshvara, which were constructed by the two chief queens of the king in memory of his conquest of Kanchi on three occasions, were profusely honoured. Two inscriptions in the Virupaksha temple record this.

The Chalukyan sculptors were no less competent in handling even the religious themes in a wordly environ.

In the field of performing arts, the Chalukyan patronage to *Bharatanāṭyaṁ* is remarkable. The sculptures of Siva as *mahānaṭa* in the Saiva *layaṇa* in Badami and the *Rāval phaḍi* cave in Aihole are the typical examples of dance forms of Siva *tāṃḍava*. Experts in *Bharatanāṭyaṁ* are able to identify the various *karaṇas* by the method of permutation and combination of each of the two hands. There is no temple in Pattadakal without the sculpture of

Siva as *mahānaṭa*. In fact, there is even a mention of a great exponent of Bharata's *nāṭyasāstra*, Natasevya by name, who is eloquently praised. There are two inscriptions in the Virupaksha temple in Pattadakal. He is eulogised thus:

Khāta- mahāprabhāva –Bharat-āgama- yukti- bahu-prakā-
rada mātinoḷ-ella mēṇ Naṭasevyana munte yathō-
kta-mārgadind-ī-teṛad-iḷdud-agra- tala –sancaram-embu-
d-id-endu-dē(pē)ḷdoḍe-inn-ātane nartakaṃ naṭa-
roḷargalaṃ-ī bhuvan-antar-ā[ḷa]doḷ Dēvayya-
gaḷā maga Acalan

The other inscription is all praise for Natasevya. Being an extraordinary expert in and an authority on Bharata's *Natyasaṣtra*, and strictly following the *sastra*, he is like a lion humbling proud elephant like other so-called dance experts, who think themselves to be great in the art, etc.

4. Literary activity was probably at its height during the Chalukyan period. Pulakesi II's son, Chandraditya's wife, Vijaya Bhattarika herself was a poetess of distinction known for her *Vaidarbhi* style, next to Kalidasa—an exceptionally eminent poet in the history of Sanskrit literature. Rajasekhara, a great rhetorician of the 11th century, openly acknowledges and praises her eminence in the usage of *Vaidarbhi* style and personality.

The well-known Aihole *prashasti* in Sanskrit, a masterpiece, was composed by Ravikirti, who claims to be no less great and compares himself to Kalidasa, who is well known especially for his drama *Abhijnana Shankutalam* and Bharavi reputed for his great work *Kiratarjuniyam.* These are two exceptionally great poets in Sanskrit literature. Experts after going through the *prashasti* rightly think that he was really a great poet. Ravikirti was a poet in the court of Pulakesi II.

These are some of the highlights and the soul of the Chalukyan history and culture that people would certainly appreciate and remember for long. Some more instances may be culled out from inscriptions and other sources. My intention here is not to multiply such examples but to bring home the idea enunciated in the beginning with a few examples.

All these would mean that a thorough study of the history and culture of an area or region or state or country is needed so that one may be able to select judiciously such instances that can be illustrated. It is for this purpose that this seminar has been arranged to make people understand intimately the different aspects of the history and culture of the Chalukyas.

2

The Pre-Chalukyan Cultural Scenario of Badami-Pattadakal-Aihole

A. Sundara

The natural environment of the region of Badami, Pattadakal and Aihole located on the left bank of the river Malaprabha, rich in flora and fauna, comprising long hill ranges of the sedimentary rocks (of the Kaladgi series) had been the most inviting for humans from the remotest past. Rough and heavy stone tools made on quartzite sandstone readily available on hand, belonging to the earliest stage of the Old Stone Age, i.e. Early Palaeolithic of about 5 to 10 lakh years old, had been traced years back in the areas of all the three localities. Small flakes and very tiny stone tools made of fine grained rock materials, such as jasper, chert, chalcedony, agate belonging to two subsequent stone ages—the upper Palaeolithic (*c.* 50,000–10,000 BCE) and the Mesolithic (*c.* 10,000–3000 BCE)—as well as very interesting and important cave paintings more or less of the same period also are located in Badami, Aihole and in a few other localities, such as Kutakankeri, nearby (Fig. 2.1). Remains of the settlements of the Protohistoric, Neolithic in the Chalcolithic stage (*c.* 3000 to 800 BCE) are located in two of these localities—Badami and Pattadakal. Rude stone chambers serving as family vaults for burial, commonly known as megaliths in archaeology, belonging to the Iron Age communities

Fig. 2.1. Prehistoric paintings in Badami region.

(*c.* 1500–300/200 BCE) also are found numerously in Pattadakal and Aihole and the nearby localities: Akkaragal, Kyaddigeri, Chelapur, Siddhanakolla and Kutakankeri. Here are found hundreds of megaliths. Each megalithic chamber is a family vault. It is interesting to note that the megalithic burial chambers are of two distinct and principal types: the porthole and the passage chambers are found in the sites as if forecasting the subsequent development of two distinct temple architectural forms of the historical period in these localities. It is these megalith builders that developed iron technology, such as mining, smelting and smithy. Large production of iron and the manufacture of tools and equipment of various kinds brought quick change in the lifestyle and also increased wealth and prosperity. Even the oral tradition prevailing in these localities speaking about the age-old Agastya, the great *maharshi* and his subjugation of Ilvala, a wealthy merchant, and his brother Vatapi, who were demonic in their lifestyle, living respectively at Aihole and Badami, look like a popular version in Puranic style about the protohistoric communities in the region. It seems to imply a steady progress, perhaps owing to some external stimulus, towards semi-urbanised cultural stages and eventually to the highly urbanised cities and towns. In fact, Badami and Pattadakal as commercial centres are referred to in Ptolemy's *A Guide to Geography* of the 2nd century CE.

The remains of the urban settlements with brick structures, etc. are traced in these localities datable to around the beginning of the CE. In 2003–2005, excavations in Pattadakal by the Archaeological Survey of India, Dharwad Circle, have revealed a continuous progress and development from advanced semi-urbanised Iron Age megalithic to the highly advanced urban centre, politically well organised under a feudatary of the Satavahana ruling dynasty around the beginning of the Current Era. This was immediately followed by the early Kadambas (*c.* 340–540 CE). In the excavations at Pattadakal, was found a large brick structure of the period (immediately following the Iron Age cultural phase), probably religious, displaying a prototype ground plan of the Sangamesvara, Virupaksha and the Mallikarjuna temples of the period of Chalukya Vijayaditya (*c.* 691–732) and Vikramaditya II (*c.* 733–743). Numerous brick structures, small as well as large, many of which enshrining *Sivalinga* or Tirthamkara stone image, stylistically of the Kadamba period, are found in Hosa-Mahakuta, Pattadakal and Aihole. Hosa-Mahakuta and the nearby Hale-Mahakuta, of fascinating natural scenic beauty, were great Saiva centres probably of the Pashupata sect.

Pattadakal, where the river Malaprabha takes a northward turn, therefore was believed to be a very sacred spot from very early times. Here for the coronation ceremony of the ruling dynasties of even the past including the Nandas of Magadha in the north and even a few of the Puranic kings such as Nahusha are traditionally believed to have had their coronation ceremony celebrated here. In Aihole, there was a strong merchant guild that in course of time became most powerful in south India known as *Ayyavole Ainurvaru.*

Naturally, the region interspersed with long high hill ranges, as if forming formidable natural fortifications, thus protective and beneficial, economically well developed and religiously sacred was found to be the most suitable and warmly inviting for the politically ambitious Chalukyas to seek their fortune and to realise their ambition. As a result, Badami became eventually the capital of a vast kingdom extending from the Narmada to the Kaveri.

Badami, Pattadakal and Aihole are very well known all over the world for the magnificent temples of great variety belonging to the early Chalukya period. In view of the many architectural forms of the temples in their early stages in these places, art historians exclaimed the places as the "laboratory of Indian temples" and also as "the cradle of Indian temple architecture." The two early main models of the temples that were adapted most commonly in the south and the north continuously through the centuries, are geographically the southern and the northern; historically Indo-Aryan and the Dravidian and architecturally *Vimana* and *Rekha Nagara*, as for example respectively the Sangameshvara and the Galaganatha in Pattadakal.

3

The Name and Home of the Early Chalukyas

S.V. Padigar

The inscriptions of the early Chalukyas found so far are entirely silent on the issues of the name and home of the dynasty. It is only in the records of the Chalukyas of Kalyana and of the later Chalukyas of Vengi that efforts were made by the composers to reflect on these points. The composers of the Vengi Chalukya records from 10th century AD onwards fabricated a myth to explain the origin of the Chalukyas. According to this, the genealogy of the ancestors of the Chalukyas goes back to Brahma. After Puranic personalities like Pururavas and Ayu, in that line, was King Udayana, who became the first of the fifty-nine kings who ruled in succession at Ayodhya. After them, several rulers succeeded and one of them was Vijayaditya. In a bid to conquer the Daksinapatha, Vijayaditya lost his life in a battle with Trilochana-Pallava, leaving behind his pregnant queen. She was rescued and given shelter by a pious Brahmana named Visnuvardhana. When the boy had come of age, he was informed of the cause of his father's death and of the events which followed it. The young prince Visnuvardhana, having vowed to regain the lost royal status, proceeded to a hill called Chalukya for performing penance. He fulfilled his ambition by the grace of the Goddess

Nanda (Gauri), and gods Kumara and Narayana, and the divine mother. He then conquered the Kadamba, Ganga and other rulers and became the master of Daksinapatha comprising seven-and-a-half lakh villages and hamlets. The son of this Visnuvardhana and of his queen of Pallava descent was Vijayaditya. Pulakesi-vallabha was his son. According to this myth, the dynasty owes its name to the Chalukya hill where Visnuvardhana assumed the insignia of sovereignty.[1]

A different myth is registered in some records of the Chalukyas of Kalyana. According to it, once while God Brahma was engaged in *Sandhya* rituals, Indra approached him with a request to create a hero who could vanquish the growing evil on the earth. Brahma looked steadily into the water of oblation in his palm (*culuka-jala*) and suddenly there sprang a great hero, the progenitor of the Chalukyas. The dynastic name Chalukya was thus derived from *culuka* of palm.[2] Ramesh observes that grammatically the derivation of Chalukya or Chalukya from *culuka* cannot be sustained.[3] The Chalukyas of Anihilavada also concocted a similar story. According to it, when Brahma was churning his *culuka,* viz. the ocean, a warrior sprang forth from it ready to obey his commands. He named the warrior as Chalukya.[4]

Both these myths do not stand scrutiny because of the contradiction in explaining the origin of the word Chalukya. On the face of it, the myth contained in the *Vengi Chalukya* records seems to have been inspired from the memories of the protracted Chalukya-Pallava conflict that emanated from the time of Pulakesi II, whose brother Visnuvardhana was the founder of the Vengi Chalukya line. The second explanatation is as mythical as the first to be true. As such, both these claims rightly stand discarded by scholars as unhistorical.

More than that, what counters these myths is the fact that in the genuine records of the Badami house, the dynasty is not referred to as Chalukya. It occurs first as Chalikya or Chalkya and later as Chalukya. This is the reason why J.F. Fleet[5] and following him N.L. Rao and R.S. Panchamukhi[6] preferred to call them Chalukyas. R.S. Panchamukhi in a later work chose to call them Chalukyas of Badami.[7] But for these few exceptions cited above, the scholars have been consistently using the form Chalukya to designate the family. In the present volume, we have preferred to use Chalukya instead of Chalukya because most inscriptions of the dynasty address it by that name. As late as the 10th century AD, even Pampa, the author of the Kannada work *Vikramarjuna-vijayam*, calls them Chalukyas.[8] As argued by Ramesh, the later descendants of this Chalukya house, who for historical reasons lost political hold for some generations, called themselves the Chalukyas or Chalukya after revival first as feudatories and later as imperial rulers. This phenomenon is noticed also in the case of the families which claimed descent from the Kadamba dynasty of Banavasi, like those of Goa and Hanagal, who are regularly addressed in their epigraphs as Kadambas or Kadambas. Ironically, in these cases scholars have been using the name Kadamba instead of Kadamba to these families. As N.L. Rao points out,[9] the stories cited in later records must have originated in about the 10th century AD, when the true significance of the name of the family had been forgotten.

Nandimath points out that the original name of the family was Chaluki, Chalki or Saluki, Salki, the last of which in Kannada means a spade.[10] Salkeppa (Salki+appa) occurs as proper name of a person, in Karnataka. On this analogy, he proposed that the Chalukyas were originally agriculturists who came to have political hold in due course and when they obtained sovereignty, stories were invented to give Puranic credence. It is difficult to pass a final word of judgement in respect of this proposition. But from the evidence of Nagarjunakonda inscription and of the Aihole inscription, it would appear that a long time had elapsed since their embracing the *ksatra-vrtti*.

Before shifting over to the question of the original home of the family, we may mention an earlier reference to family whose name resembles that early form of the name of the Chalukya house, viz. Chalikya. A Prakrit inscription of the lksvakus of Nagarjunakonda of 2nd century AD refers to a *mahasenapati mahatalavara* Khanda-Caliki Rananaka described as Vasithiputa (Vasisthiputra).[11] What comes in the way of relating Khanda-Caliki to the Chalukyas of Badami is the fact that the latter called themselves *Haritiputras* and not as *Vasisthiputras*. It becomes clear from the Chalukya records that there were other Calikya or Calki chiefs in different parts of the kingdom. Mangalesa's Nerur plates state that he had killed a Calikya chief Svamiraja, who had been victorious in eighteen battles. Similarly, we may point out here the names of Calki Lemruraju and Calki Mutturaju appearing in the reigns of Vinayaditya and Vijayaditya. They figure as petty local chiefs. Hence, in the existing state of our knowledge, it would not be appropriate to construe a direct connection between the person named in the Nagarjunakonda inscription with the Chalukyas of Badami.

THEIR ORIGINAL HOME

A second issue relating to the Chalukyas of Badami is that of their original home. Their records are again silent on this issue. Panchamukhi believed that there may be truth in the later Chalukya claim regarding their descent from the kings of Ayodhya.[12] He cites from the Aihole Inscription, which after eulogising Chalukya Satyasraya goes on to state that after him in that family there were many victorious kings who reigned (*tad-vamsesu jigisusu tesu bahusv-apy-atitesu*). This reference here, according to him, may be to those rulers who ruled probably in the north. K.V. Ramesh has further developed this argument.[13] The Sanjan copperplate charter of Rashtrakuta Amoghavarsa I, in the context of eulogising Krishna I, refers to the Chalukya king as 'elevated by means of the throne of Ayodhya and chowries'(*Ayodhya-simhasana-chamar-orjitah*).[14] Taking this as clue together with the claims made in the records of the later Chalukyas of Vengi and of Kalyana, Ramesh has argued that the Chalukyas originally hailed from Ayodhya region and that they migrated en mass accompanied by families and individuals drawn from all sections of society, of both sexes and of all ages, from all the four castes and from outside, from all the professions and crafts" including "skilled architects and sculptors, artisans and stone-mesons." He further argues that this explains many Chalukya temples have incorporated northern style of architecture.[15] It is difficult to agree with this postulation basically because no such claim of Ayodhya connection is made in any record of the Badami Chalukya dynasty. Further, the 'nothern 'features are not discernible in early architectural products of the Chalukyas, such as Cave I and II or the Upper and Lower Sivalayas at Badami, assigned to 6th century AD. On the other hand, they conform to Dravida or 'southern' tradition. Ramesh's futher argument that the Chalukyas made their way to Deccan via Gujarat is based on the Kaira plates of Vijayaraj,[16] the grandson of Jayasimha, dated year 394. Like Fleet,[17] Ramesh takes the year to be in Saka era and equates it to AD 472-73. This epigraph mentions Vijayaraja as the son of Vallabha–Ranavikranta Buddhavarama and grandson of Jayasimha of Chalukya dynasty. He identifies this Jayasimha with the grandfather of Pulakesi I. If we accept his view, Vijayaditya of the Kaira Plates would be a cousin of Pulakesi I. But from all that we know, the difference of dates between Vijayaditya and Pulakesi would be about 70 years. Although Ramesh tries to set aside this problem of difference of decades, it is indeed difficult to justify this difference. If the Kaira copperplate charter was the earliest record of the dynasty, one would have expected to find the name of the family mentioned in it as Chlikya or Chalkya, as it occurs in the early records. This is not the case. There is also the problem of the certainty of identifying the era used therein with the Saka era. Mirashi feels that the grant is spurious and the era used therein is the Kalacuri–Chedi era or the Gupta era. In that case, the date of the record would be AD 642-43.[18] On the basis of a comparison of other epigraphs contemporary to the Chalukyas, he shows that the format is unlike that of the Chalukyan, that it draws from Kalacuri and other dynastic records of the 7th century AD and that names of a number of donees appearing in the record are the same as those appearing in the Kaira plates of Dadda II, which was also found together with the record attributed to Jayasimha's grandson Chalukya Vijayaditya. Thus, he considers it as spurious. Against this background, the Kaira plates of Chalukya Vijayaditya cannot be relied upon for historical information.

In the present state of our knowledge, it would be appropriate to look into the Chalukya records themselves to find out what they imply in terms of their geographical affiliation at the time of their ascent. By a careful study of the epigraphs, N.L. Rao has long ago pointed out certain facts that hint at the Chalukya homeland. The Rashtrakuta inscriptions refer to the Chalukyas as Karnataka's, i.e. belonging to Kannada-speaking country, which implies that they identified themselves as natives of that country (*Kancisa-Kerala-naradhipa-Cola-Pandya-Sri-Harsa-Vajrata-Vibeda-vidhana daksham Karnatakam balam-anatam-ajeyam-anyair-bhartyaih kiyadbhir-api yah sahasa jigaya*). The names of some of the rulers of the family end in a typical Kannada regal suffix *arasa,* which stands for the Sanskrit word *raja* (king). For example, Kirtivarma I is referred to as Katti–*arasa* in Godachi charter, while the seal of the Satara charter of Yuvaraja Visnuvardhana, the younger brother of Pulakesi II, gives his name as Bittarasa. Likewise, Manor plates of Vinayaditya Mangalarasa of Gujarat branch of the family mentions the prince as Mangalarasaraja. Many more such instances can be added to this list. The fact that the suffix *arasa* figures even in Sanskrit inscriptions shows that the Chalukyas had become identified with Kannada-speaking land by the time they ascended to power. Names of some of the Chalukya rulers also are of Kannada origin. For instance, the name of the founder of the Badami house, Pulakesi I. There are other forms of this name, like Pulikesi, Pulekesi and Pulekesi. But the original name, as pointed out by Fleet, is Pulikesi.[19] This, according to N.L. Rao, is a Kannada name which means 'one who resembled Krishna in prowess from babyhood.'[20] Likewise, the real name of Kirtivarma I was Katti-arasa, again a Kannada name. In this, *katti* means sword and *arasa* means king. Bittarasa is another such name which is the Kannada form of Vishnuraja. Chalukyas used Kannada for some inscriptions issued by them outside their empire, as for instance the Kanci inscription of Vikramaditya II. This suggests that they gave official status to the Kannada language, though their copperplate charters are in Sanskrit.

Of course, the Kannada-speaking geographical area then meant the region between the rivers Godavari and Kaveri, as defined by Srivijaya, the author of *Kavirajamargam*.[21] However, we must emphasise that the Chalukyas belonged to the upper part of this geographical area, comprising of the present-day southern Maharashtra and northen Karnataka, or the region between the Godavari and the Krishna. Perhaps the Jamalagama grant of Vijayaditya seems to be of greater significance in this respect. It referes to Callumki-desa in which was the grant village Jamalagama, located between Pullavadali and Mugali on the western side of Morakhandi. Of these places, Morakhandi has been indetified with Morakhandi in Bidar district in Karnataka and the remaining villages are identified in the neighbouring Latur district in Maharashtra. Accordingly, Callumki-desa would correspond to the present-day Latur-Bidar area of Maharashtra-Karnataka.[22] In the Tumbeyanuru grant, the grant village is stated to have been situated in the Chalukya-visaya. The grant villages are not identified properly, but one suggestion is that they should be in the region of the confluence of the rivers Tungabhadra and Krishna.[23] This would be roughly the Kurnool-Mahbubnagar region. The question whether we have to take that the region was named Chalukya-visaya after they added it to their kingdom or because it was their homeland, is difficult to answer. Of course, this too was a part of the Kannada-speaking zone as the numerous Kannada inscriptions of the Chalukya period found there show. D.P. Dikshit also supports this argument when he says, "The Chalukyan homeland was somewhere on the border between Maharashtra and Karnataka."[24]

THE QUESTION OF FORMER OVERLORDS

Who were the overlords of the Chalukyas before they assumed sovereignty? Most scholars writing on the history of the Chalukyas have taken for granted that as chiefs they served under the Kadambas of Banavasi before becoming independent. As a support to this, the stylistic similarity in the epigraphs of the two dynasties is cited. But none of the inscriptions in this volume contributes to this belief. On the other hand, an examination of the early records implies that they had no encounter with the Kadambas during the establishment of their dynastic rule. Pulakesi I's Badami cliff inscription only refers to his performing *Asvemedha* and other Vedic rituals and turning Vatapi hill into an impregnable fort. The

Aihole inscription of Pulakesi II gives to Pulakesi I the credit of performing the *Asvamedha* and other sacrifices and of making Vatapipuri the capital, but does not mention his encounter with any contemporary dynasty. On the other hand, the Chalukya encounter with the Kadambas finds first mention only in connection with Kirtivarma I. Later inscriptions of the Chalukyas also do not preserve any tradition of the Chalukyas being the feudatories of the Kadambas. It would appear from the analysis of the early Kadamba records that to them the regions of Bijapur and Bagalkot and beyond to the east and north were of marginal interest. For this reason, when Pulakesi I fortified Vatapi, the Kadamabas, engaged in internecine struggles, seem to have remained indifferent. Their indifference soon cost them their sovereignty. That the Kadambas were fragmented into branches is clearly indicated by the Aihole inscription, which refers to the felling of the 'host of the branches of the Kadamba tree' by Kirtivarma I (*prthu-kadamba-kadamba-kadamakam*).

The later Chalukya tradition favours the view that earlier they were the subordinates of the Rashtrakutas. On the evidence of Undikavatiaka grant, Panchamukhi[25] and Dikshit[26] have argued that Jayasimha, the grandfather of Pulakesi I, was in charge of the Harivatsa fort as subordinate of Abhimanyu of the Rashtrakuta family of Manapura. It is possible that this Chalukya chief defeated one of the members of the Rashtrakuta family. Apart from the Manapura family, there appear to have been several branches of Rashtrakuta family. Dejja-Maharaja of Gokak plates, whom Ramesh holds to be one of the victims of Pulakesi I, was also of Rashtrakuta stock.[27] The encounter of Pulakesi II with Govinda and Appayika suggests the presence of the Rashtrakutas in the Deccan region.

NOTES AND REFERENCES

1. *IA.* XIV, p.48; *SII.* Vol.I, pp.53-54; B.R. Gopal *et al.* (ed.), *Epigraphical Studies (introduction and papers of N.L. Rao)*, p. 254.
2. K.V. Ramesh, *The Chalukyas of Vatapi*, p. 14.
3. *Ibid.*
4. *IA.* Vol. XII, pp. 201ff.
5. J.F. Fleet, *Dynasties of the Kanarese Districts.*

6. N.L. Rao and R.S. Panchamukhi, *Karnatakada Arasumanetanagalu*, pp. 45ff.
7. R.S. Panchamukhi, *Karnatakada Itihasa*, Vol. I, pp. 131ff.
8. *Vikramarjunavijayam, Asvasa* I, V.
9. B.R. Gopal *et al. op. cit.*, p. 254.
10. *KTA.*, p. 198.
11. *EI.* Vol. XX, pp. 1ff.
12. R.S. Panchamukhi, *op. cit.*, pp. 142-44.
13. K.V. Ramesh, *op. cit.* pp.19-23.
14. *Ibid.*, p. 19; This Expression had been translated by Bhandarakar as 'elevated by incontestable throne and chowries'.
15. *Ibid.*, p. 20.
16. *JRAS.* (New Series), Vol. I, pp. 242-51.
17. *IA.* Vol. VII, p. 242; later Fleet discarded his view.
18. *CII.* Vol. IV, pt. I, pp. 167-68.
19. *Dynasties of Kanarese Districts*, p. 343, fn.5.
20. *Pole* means impurity of childbirth, i.e. of the natal chamber. *Kesi* is an alternative name of Kesava, i.e. Krsna. Gopal B.R. *et al.*, *op. cit.*, p. 255.
21. *Kavirajamargam*, I, 36.
22. However, S.H. Ritti tells me that the correct reading of the administrative division could be Bhallumkidesa, and that referes to an administrative divison with Bhalki in Bidar district as its headquarters.
23. S.S. Ramachandra Murthy, "the Chalukyas of Vatapi/Badami", in B. Rajendra Prasad (ed.), *Early Medieval Andhra Pradesh AD 624-1000*, p. 141.
24. D.P. Dikshit, *A Political History of the Chalukyas of Badami*, pp. 25-26.
25. R.S. Panchamukhi, *op. cit.*, pp. 135-36.
26. D.P. Dikshit, *op. cit.*
27. *EI.* Vol. XXI, pp. 289-92.

4

Early Chalukya Rule in Andhradesa

Kolluru Suryanarayana

In the history of Andhradesa, the advent of the Early Chalukyas (who later established their branch in Andhra as the Chalukyas of Vengi) (AD 624–AD 1075) is significant as marking the beginning of a glorious period under which the culture of the Telugu people took its real shape. Their matchless efforts at extension of the kingdom during the period of Ranavikrama Pulakesi II, the dear brother of Kubja Vishnuvardhana, who founded the Vengi kingdom, brought the Badami Chalukyas to Andhra from the borders of Karnataka. Their march resulted in the establishment of a stable kingdom with an uninterrupted sway for more than five centuries with an unbroken line of succession. Probably, with the zeal of extension of empire, their *prasastis* claimed connection with Mahasena or Kartikeya, the God of war, as the tutelary deity of the line (*Mahasenapadanudhyatrunam*). In some of their inscriptions, they claimed to have occupied the whole earth by the fierce prowess of their own arms (*Sva-bhujavikrama-Krantamahi-bhujam*). Undoubtedly, in the series of their conquests, it became necessary for them to depend upon some of the subordinate officers and chiefs who followed them loyally and guarded their interests throughout their political career. At the time of succession, struggles in the royal family and in subduing the rebellious elements in the kingdom, those subordinate families played a decisive role in sealing their fortunes. To cite an example: in the civil war which ensued in the time of Mangalesa at Badami, it was a subordinate family of Adi Maha Bappara, which helped and supported the claims of Pulakesi II for the throne. Similarly, it would have been impossible for Pulakesi II and Kubja Vishnuvardhana to establish themselves in Andhradesa, an unfamiliar area before their conquest into those areas, without the willing support and hearty cooperation of some of the feudatory families. They seem to have brought along with them a number of military chieftains and settled them in Vengimandala, bestowed upon them rulership over different territories as rewards for their loyal military services rendered to them in the conquest of Venginadu and consolidation of the Chalukyan authority over it. The Durjaya family of the Giripaschimasima was rewarded with the hereditary rulership of some villages on the southern bank of the river Krishna. Similarly, even though it is not directly mentioned, the Matsya family to which Atavi Durjaya, a Jnapti of the Chipurupalli plates belongs, might have been also rewarded with the rulership of a small tract of the country in northern Andhra. Thus, the Chalukyas, who hailed from Karnataka, were prepared to honour and reward the services of those chieftains who loyally assisted them by bestowing upon them the rulerships over different territories in the then Vengidesa (Andhra country). This establishment of the military officers as the feudal chiefs resulted in the beginning of the Mandalika phase in the history of Andhradesa, which continued up to the expansion of Muslim power in that area, i.e. up to the end of the 16th century. Thus, the policy of conquest and consolidation of authority as well as the establishment of *mandalika* powers which served the Badami Chalukyas with unsullied loyalty and unflinching dedication have given rise to a new significant chapter in the history of Telugunadu.

In the Aihole *prasasti*, Ravikirthi beautifully described the conquest of various provinces in the Vengi and Kalinga Kingdoms by Pulikesin II. Basing upon the various inscriptional evidences, a number of scholars like J.F. Fleet, V. Rangacharya, N. Venkataramanaya, B.V. Krishna Rao, Ganguly, M. Somasekhara Sarma and some others thoroughly discussed the date as well as the political circumstances under which this area was conquered by the Chalukyas of Badami.

Different inscriptions of the period describe the course of events thus:

> Through the excellences of their householders, prominent in the pursuit of the three objects of life and having broken the pride of other rulers of the earth, the Kalingas with the Kosalas by his (Pulakesin II's) army were made to evince signs of fear.
>
> Hard pressed (*pists*) by Him, Pistapura became a fortress not difficult of access; wonderful to relate, the ways of the Kali Age to him were quite inaccessible!
>
> Ravaged by him, the water of Kunala—coloured with the blood of men killed with many weapons, and the land within it overspread with arrays of accoutred elephants—was like the cloud—covered sky in which the red evening twilight has risen.
>
> (*Aihole Inscription, E.I.,* Vol. VI, p. 11).

> His Satyasraya I; son was the famous Kirttivarman (I) .... His son (is) one of great splendour ......By him, the favourite of fortune and of the earth, the Yuvaraja Visnuvardhana (I), (also called) Visamasiddhi.... Stationed at Karumarathi (or Karumarathya).... On the full-moon tithi of the month Karttika, there has been given..... the village named Alanda-tirtha in the Srinilayabhoga, on the north of the *agrahara* of Anopalya and on the bank of the Bhimarathi ... to Acalasvamin, Vedasvamin, and Devasvamin, together with Adityasvamin and Nagakumara.
>
> (*Satara Grant, I.A.,* Vol. XIX, p. 310)

The glorious Pulakesi—Prithvivallabha—Maharaja, (who) like (his) father (is) a hero, the abode of truth (Satyasraya), whose commands are unopposed suitably honours (the officials of this district and informs them as follows):

> Be it known (to you that), Vallabha, being present in person, the execution (of the present grant) was formally bestowed on Prithviduvaraja, (i.e. Prithiviyuvaraja) who, having defeated the circle of enemies by his arm which was a churning-stick of the wicked (people) of the Kali (age), which was skilled in daring deeds in many battles, (and) which was wielding the drawn sword, has secured the kingdom to the lineage of his son.

(*Kopparam Plates, E.I.*, Vol. XVIII, p. 260).

> His Satyasraya's younger brother, the renowned lord, named Visnuvardhana, destroyed the Durjayas and obtained Vengi-mandala

(*Katlaparru Grant*, S.V.T.V.N Hindu High School Annual, 1939-40, p. 24).

> That king of incomparable strength, having driven out the Durjayas who had occupied the Andhra-Visaya, obtained the Vengi country for the first time and made it his own.

(*Pandipaka Grant*, Elliot's Collection, 15-6-26, p. 185).

> In the beginning, Kubja-Vishnuvardhana by the prowess resembling that of Visnu wrested this earth forcibly from Durjaya and ruled it for eighteen years.

(*Kandyam Plates, JAHRS*, Vol. XI, p. 85).

By the above information, it is clear that this branch of Chalukyas founded by Kubja Vishnuvardhana, the beloved brother of Pulakesi II at Vengi in Andhradesa, is an offshoot family of the Badami Chalyukyas. The affection and love of Pulakesi II towards his brother Kubja Vishnuvardhana is well attested to in the records of the Chalukyas. It seems that along with Pulakesi II, his 'priyanuja' Kubja Vishnu also died in the battlefield in the battles with the Pallavas, as no record of him is available after that date.

From the period of Jayasimha I, the son and successor of Kubja Vishnu, though did not acknowledge the parental home

Badami in their records, practically they followed the administrative policy of the Early Chalukyas. In claiming their origin and early home as well as in bearing the titles, they totally followed the Badami line. Until their advent into the Telugu country, Telugu people had no literature of their own and no sculpture of their own. To say, what is known as Andhra culture today is no other than the legacy of that offshoot Badami line. They founded a number of villages and habitations in Andhra, promoted or constructed a number of temples in Andhra. They considered battle as a necessary evil for the expansion of the empire, and hence where they fought, immediately after that battle, they used to construct a Siva temple in that place. Vijayaditya fought 108 battles and constructed 108 Siva temples. Chalukya Bhima I fought 360 battles and constructed 360 Siva temples. Majority of the ancient Siva temples that were constructed in Andhra at various places like Dhaksharama, Samarlakot, Palakollu, Bikkavolu, and Vijayawada were undoubtedly their contribution. Telugu language, Telugu stanzas, and Telugu literature flourished and promoted under their patronage. Only due to their Badami connections, there existed harmony between Kannada and Andhra cultures. They promoted education by their liberal grants to *ghatikas* like Sanapura. Following the footprints of the first Kannada *kavya* of Pampa, roughly a century later the Telugus also created the first *kavya* of their own under the patronage of Chalukya Rajaraja. It is also surmised that the Chalukyan emperor Gunaga Vijayaditya of the Vengi Branch had written a book in Kannada by name *Gunagankiyam,* which is referred to in a Tamil work *Yapparilingarikkai Chchandai.* Thus, the cultural affinity between Telugu and Kannada continued in south India due to the rule of Chalukyan lineages originally originated at Badami.

BIBLIOGRAPHY

Fleet, J.F., *Dynasties of the Kanarese Districts*, Bombay Gazetteer, Vol. I, Part 11, Bombay, 1806.

Ganguly, D.C., *Eastern Chalukyas*, Banaras, 1937.

Venkatakrishna Rao, B., *History of Eastern Chalukyas of Vengi*, Hyderabad, 1973.

Venkataramayayya, N., *The Eastern Calukyas of Vengi*, Madras, 1950.

——, *Pallavulu-Chalukyulu*, (Telugu), Madras, 1969.

Journals:

Andhra Sahitya Parishad Patrika.

Bharati.

Epigraphia Indica.

Indian Antiquary.

Journal of Andhra Historical Research Society.

5

Chalukyas and Jainism

Nagarajaiah, Hampa (Hampana)

The Chalukyas, a celebrated ancient dynasty in the south, ruled from 6th to 8th century AD. They projected Karnataka on a wider canvas by their military power, administrative ability and socio-cultural contributions. The remains of age-old forts, the cave temples and the inscriptions beam floodlight on its past glory.

The Chalukyas established a new empire with Badami as its axis. Pulakesin held his own empire only to the north of the Vindhyas. More than the Kadambas of Banavasi and the Gangas, it was the Chalukyas who waged a series of successful wars against other neighbours in the north and south. The Chalukyas rightly earned the rare distinction of bringing the two territories of the Adigangas under the sway of a single Belgode (*Svetachatra*), 'the royal white parasol', and enlarging its boundaries by ably annexing large parts of the Deccan, and eventually many more petty principalities merged into the mighty Chalukyan monarchy.

The *Durgas*, 'Forts', in Karnataka are classified into four types, namely *Jaladurga* (Water Fort), *Giridurga* (Hill Fort), *Vanadurga (*Forest Fort) and *Neladurga (*Ground Fort). The forts at Badami are examples of *Giridurga* type, i.e. hill forts.

The two strong forts on the two hills, on the outskirts of Badami town proper, stretch, one to the north and the other to the south. In the common parlance, these forts are called *Bavanbande Kote* (the Fifty-two Rocks Fort), and the *Ranamandala Kote* (the Battlefield Fort), respectively. A large lake, in between the two hills, may be as ancient as the forts, if not the hills!

The forts at Badami are good examples of the ancient type of forts, built upon large rocks joined by masonry, extant in Deccan. Pulakesin I, the early architect of the fort, built it in AD 543, on the middle portion of the sloping hill, and as such it had the charming look of a hanging fort. Later, their successors, the Rashtrakutas, also added and extended these forts.

The Chalukyas, an indigenous *Kula*, emerged from their obscurity, thanks to the valorous Jayasimha, foregoer. Jayasimha, grandfather of Pulakesin I, feudatory of Abhimanyu, overthrew and wrested the kingdom of Manapur. The Rashtrakutas, by defeating Indra, son of Krisna Dejja Maharaja, grandson of Krisna and probably son of Indra, had shouldered suzerainty of the Chalukyas. History repeated, after two hundred years, and once again the Rashtrakutas recovered the kingdom that they had lost. Earlier they had lost a small province, but now Dantidurga and his son recovered a vast kingdom, as though collecting the principal with compound interest! Subsequently, it rose to become an imperial dynasty, by the might and brilliance of successive rulers, who acted as trophic nerves of a robust empire. It is well known that many of the later Chalukya inscriptions are dated in the regnal years of chief rulers. The distinction of the first mention of the Saka era by name in Karnataka goes to the Badami Rock-cliff inscription of Pulakesin I, dated Saka 465 (AD 543), recording the fortification of the Hill of Vatapi by that king. Elsewhere, the earliest being the Hisse Borla inscription of Devasena, the Vakataka chief, which mentions the Saka year 380, equivalent to AD 458.

So far we have taken cognizance of the fact that among the celebrated dynasties that ruled Karnataka, the Chalukyas of Badami were an all-powerful radiant dynasty. They built a potent and efficient dynasty, who were invincible for over two hundred years. The Chalukya troops formed the vanguard of the Karnataka army. Poets and epigraphs make references to the reign of Pulakesin

II, strongly tinged with the mythology of the concept of *Chakravarti*, the wheel-emperor. Similarly, it is also remarkable that they were the earliest architects of fame. Art, architecture and literature blossomed under their umbrella. They disseminated their domination beyond the boundaries, extending the culture of Karnataka up to South-East Asia. The Chalukyas of Kalyana, Vengi, and Vemulada were the later branches of this main stalk.

Hereditary monarchy was the prevailing form of government and the line of succession accorded preference to the eldest son. When succession to the throne failed in the main male line, then the inevitable choice would be in favour of the most deserved under the circumstances, ability and character being the main criterion/touchstone. For instance, Vikramaditya I, though was fourth of the five sons of Pulakesin II, by virtue of skill and might, occupied the Chalukya throne.

Pulakesin II, hailed as *daksinapatha-prithivyahsvāmi* with full regalia of imperial titles of—*Satyaśraya Srîpṛithvî-Vallabha Mahārājādhiraja-Paramēśvara-Bhaṭṭāraka,* ruled like a wheel emperor with Karnataka region forming the central core of *Cakravartiksetra*. Then on, the emperor of Karnatakadesa came to be known by the non-dynastic cognomen of Vallabha the paramount and the imperial army begot the non-dynastic designation of *Karnata-bala*. Thus, the Karnataka empire remained more or less a constant factor and only different royal dynasties replaced one another to rule the readymade Karnataka empire.

The exit of Pulakesin II created a political vacuum. However, putting an end to the turbid political geography of Karnatakadesa, the self-confident Vikramaditya I once again revived power to give it a unitary shape and re-establish the Chalukya hegemony.

Clamping his suzerainty, he brought many minor principalities under a single Chalukya umbrella. The Chalukyas, anxious to wipe out the disgrace of defeat, were forced to live in *ajnatavasa* incognito for a stretched period of two centuries to recoup and come back with added strength to retaliate. Surprisingly, their latent imperial potential surfaced at the appropriate opportune to overpower and crush the Rashtrakutas. The Chalukyas achieved imperial aura of becoming overlords of a vast territory bounded by four oceans and open a new chapter of golden era from late 10th century to late 12th century.

The honorific subtitles of *Ranadhira,* the valiant in battle and *Raṇarāga,* he who delights in war, were employed by the Chalukyas and the Santaras. Their feudatories, possibly the Pandyas of Tamil Nadu also fond of this appellation, were the earliest to use this epithet as part of their nomenclature. We may cite the name of Sadiyan Koccadaiyan Ranadhira (794–800), son of Arikesari Asamasama Maravarman Ranaraga.

The history of the Chalukyas may facilitate the antiquarian for further researches on political, socio-religious conditions and on the history of art, archaeology and literature. During the period certain personal names were made popular with either abbreviated or variant forms. For instance, Vikramaditya, son of Somesvara I, was known as Vikki. Similarly, Vikramaditya, son of Vijayditya, was known as Bikki. Kirtivarman had the alias of Kattiarasa and Kartavirya had the aliases of Kattama/Katta.

The Chalukyas enjoyed the distinction of establishing good administration and cordial relations with their neighbours, which continued to be a model tradition for their successors.

The Chalukyas were the pioneers to initiate the practice of entertaining a poet-laureate at each important king's court. Ravikirti was the first and paramount poet to become the earliest known court-poet in Karnataka. Added to the list of singularity, the Chalukyas have the distinction of animating the language and literature of *Pūrvada-Paḷagannaḍa,* i.e. pre-old-Kannada ethology.

The socio-cultural structure of this period is marked by the rulership of minor kings of regional level of unified vast empire and the warrior chiefs of local subaltern orders with their army force.

The Vatapi Chalukyas shouldered the responsibility of patronizing as well as protecting the local and substratum elements. As a popular tradition, they popularized construction of tanks and the method of *gōsāsa,* gifting thousand cows. The Shiggaon inscriptions have recorded fourteen tanks of this period. As mentioned elsewhere, Anningere in Gangavadi and Gadi Keshavara, Mallasamudra, Pattadakal, Badami and Kopana—all the places in Chalukya territory—received royal patronage to thrive as principal Jaina centres. Kirtivaman I, Vijayaditya, Vinaditya and Vikramaditya II supported Jainism with ardour. Princess Kumkuma Mahadevi and her husband, King Chiravahana, had great eclectic spirit.

True, the Kadambas had accorded an imperial status and dignity to Jainism. Albeit, we may justifiably say that the Badami monarchs not only enhanced Jainism's political stateliness but also augmented its nobility in the social scale. The depth and dimension of their involvement and their continued participation in the Jaina socio-religious and art-activities are reliably and reasonably reconstructed from recorded evidences that merit serious consideration.

The catholic policy and participation of the Chalukya rulers was such that no incident of religious discrimination or disturbance has been reported in the distinguished reign. Rightly swept up in the spirit of the age, the Chalukya kings faithfully followed the aeonial commandment, and are celebrated for their unswerving fidelity to the plighted word. Jainism made a deep penetration into the Chalukya society due to the ruler's active participation.

Jaina monks, known for their virtue and cognoscente, worked like bees for the efflorescence of Jaina *saṁgha.* Their influence on both the royal family, the elite and the people in general is notable.

Jainism, by this time, had been firmly established. The Adikadambas extended full support. Jainism had very visibly taken the *caityavāsi* or abbatial colour, character and form. The Banavasi Kadambas had proclaimed their faith in the Jaina Order:

> *Yasmin Jinēndrapūjā pravartate*
> *Tatra tatra dēśa parivṛddhihi/*
> *Nagarānām nirbhayatā taddēśa*
> *Svāminā corjā //namo namaḥ//*

> "Wheresoever worship of Jinendra is kept up, there is prosperity of the country and the cities are free from fear, and the Lords of those countries acquire strength (Reverence, reverence)".

During Chalukya age, Jainism attained further ascendence and decisively spread from urban concentration to rural parts. Several Jina and related pantheonic images datable to this regime are noticed at different and distant Jaina establishments. The art and architecture formulated and shaped through the progressive integration of the achievements of their predecessors.

The contribution of Jaina architecture and history to the cultural glory of India has been considerable and worthy of meticulous study. As handmaids of architecture, sculptures and paintings have glorified the magnificent monuments raised for Jinas and other adorable deities. Jaina art and literature took its concrete shape during the Badami Chalukya age—its range is wide, the charm inviting and the study revealing. To abbreviate, the period embodies a whole treasure-house of Jaina architecture.

During the enlightened rule of the Chalukyas, the architectural activities were at the highest point. Inscriptions allude to the construction of many temples of all isms and sects. Some epigraphs go a step further and attest to the fact that the members of the imperial house were of secular disposition. Their eminence in the field of arts and architecture is *sui generis.* The rock-cut and structural stone places of worship at Aihole, Badami, Pattadakal, the umbilicus cities of the empire, attest their devotion to religion and architecture.

In fact, the splendid rock-cut temples at Ellora, the most remarkable monuments of the Rashtrakutas, is an inspiration from the Chalukyan prototype pattern at Badami. The site is all the more vital due to its being the confluence of the three main Indian sects—the Brahmanical, Buddhist and Nirgrantha.

The Aihole Jaina cave called Meena Basadi in common parlance, situated in a secluded place, is the earliest monument that calls for special attention. It is a wonderful excavation, evidently the work of a master craftsman in this medium-large, well-planned and skillfully chiselled out of the solid rock with infinite forethought and patience. The rock-cut shrine, consisting of a central hall entered by a doorway, has a cell cut further into the rock. With its style at once original and vigorous, the rock-architecture is fully matured and marked by innovations, and the stages, if any, of its evolution are no longer traceable. Possibly, this single-storeyed rock-cut shrine has derived inspiration from two-storeyed Khandagiri and Udayagiri *gumphas*. This exceptionally vivid and spirited example of the Aihole rock-sculpture saw its culmination at Ellora, where the technical skill and artistic excellence of the great craftsman are best seen.

In the series of four caves (Nos. I to IV), the last and fourth cave occupying the northern horn of the Badami ridge is prime from the standpoint of the study of Jaina architecture and iconography of the pre-medieval times. The rock-cut hall-shrine, belonging exclusively to the Digambara *anvaya*, is datable to the last quarter of the 6th century, two hundred years earlier to the Jaina caves at Ellora.

In terms of quality and quantity, the Jaina contribution to art and architecture of the period is singular and substantial. In short, the many-splendoured effulgence of Jaina celestial panorama of the period continues to inspire and take us beyond the mundane.

The intellectual and cultural glory, and the philosophical richness of Jaina tradition did not confine only to the monks and nuns of assiduous discipline. Its impact, which pervaded on other allied branches of discipline, is worth pondering. Particularly, in the field of art and architecture, it blossomed to greater heights with the pink of perfection of aesthetic craftsmanship, and the most precious asset of Jaina monuments comes from this age. Some of the magnificent monuments raised for deities and other adorable ones during this period are treasure-houses of sculptural nuances. Literature has contributed in no small measure to the achievement of Jaina genius at the highest level. Even a bird's-eye view is sufficient to narrate an absorbing story of a panorama of Jaina architecture. To visually illustrate the delicacy of form and technique, some chosen examples can be illustrated.

The Megudi, 'the upper temple', at Aihole, solicited by Ravikirti, poet-laureate of Pulakesi II, consecrated in AD 634-35, is the earliest datable structural shrine of the Vatapi Chalukyas:

> If other temples had been built during his reign either at Badami or at Aihole, as they certainly must have been, we have no clinching epigraphical evidence to identify such

> important centres as Badami, Pattadakal, Aihole, and Alampur, had been, during the successive periods of the Rashtrakutas and Kalyana Chalukyas, renovated or repaired, with additions and alterations, and with replacements of damaged members with imitations of the originals or with those prepared in accordance with current trends, thus disturbing, in various degree, the original structures (Ramesh K.V.: 1984:97).

The inscriptions in the temples of Megudi, Lad Khan, Durga, Huccimalligudi, Jyotirlinga and Galaganatha group, Ramalingesvara and Charantimatha indicate that the method of inscribing/installing the inscriptions in the temples had become a tradition by this period. As a rare coincidence, the oldest and famous *prasasti* inscription of Pulakesin II, composed by Ravikirti, which forms a useful basis for the Chalukya history, is found in the Megudi Jinalaya.

Ambika, a prominent *sasanadevi* and supernatural of Jaina legend, seated on her throne in the celestial abode with court (i.e. in the company of her retinue and children) is *sui generis*, and the earliest in the Deccan. In the process of stylistic infiltration into the distant parts of the state, regional variations played their role. Parallel to this, the emergence of other two popular Yaksis, of Jvalamalini and Padmavati, is to be noted. Similarly, Syama, Dharenendra and Sarvanha Yaksas were also introduced in this epoch. The iconographic form of aesthetic, with the prescribed iconic norms, had reached a high water-mark, which had a direct impact on the later plastic art of Jaina deities, an eloquent testimony to the rich and brilliant craftsmanship and artistic talent of the Chalukya age. Opening a new chapter in the art history, the sculptures of Jinas and *sasanadevatas* signify the beginning of an era that provided opportunities to assimilate the alien elements, and to give vent to the indigenous sensibilities.

The Nadumba Basadi at Bijavada (Mod. Bezwada) was the Patta-Jinalaya, 'Royal temple' of the Vengi (Eastern) Chalukyas. Historians have established that the advent and success of Jaina *samgha* started from 4th and 3rd century BC. Kharavela, emperor of Kalinga (2nd BC) and a devout Jaina, popularized Jinadharma in the eastern coastal region, from Orissa to Andhra. Subsequentaly, the Chalukyas of Badami spread and strengthened the religion. Further, Jainism made its headway in the days of Eastern Chalukyas:

> The credit of fostering the *anēkantamata* goes to the Eastern Chalukya monarchs, some of whom were Jaina by persuasion. Ayyana Mahadevi, the queen of King Visnuvardhana III of that family, renewed in Saka 684 (AD 762) an earlier grant of a village named Musinikunda (location given) to the Jaina temple Nadumba basadi at Bijavada through the teacher Kalibhadracarya of the Kavaruri *gana* and the *Sanghanvaya* (Saletore; 251).

CEILING DECORATION

The sculptures on the ceiling have certain characteristics that correspond to the common and favourite themes of the period. At the same time, the decorative sculptures show some features that belong exclusively to the religion to which the shrine is excavated or commissioned.

The ceiling of the rectangular *Vithika* in the Meena Basadi *olim* Jain cave at Aihole, measuring 10.43 m x 2.63 m, and 2.46 m high from the floor level, is embellished with popular motifs of the contemporary period. It is mainly decorated with flower and other elaborate, decorative designs. A large blooming lotus, with three rows of petals in the centre of an excellently bordered rectangular frame, is followed with four more lotus medallions at the corners. Floral designs, a pair of fishes with floriated tails, *makaras*, and other patterns of auspicious objects, cover the space between the lotuses. The border of the central lotus hub has rosettes. The designed structures lack the plasticity of the subsequent period. The auspicious mark of *Svastika* is carved on the ceiling in the porch of the Aihole Jaina cave.

Chronological Chart of Jaina Monuments and Sculptures:

1. Aduru: Jinendra Bhavan: AD 700
2. Aihole: Jaina Cave: AD 580
   Jinendra Bhavan (Megudi): AD 634-35
   Two Minor Caves: Early 7th Century

Ambika Image: AD 635
Jvalamalini and Syama Yaksa Images: Late 7th Century

3. Annigeri (AnnigeRe): Chedia: AD 751-52
4. Badami: Jaina Cave: AD 590-95
5. Bejavada: Nedumbivasati: Early 7th Century
6. Bhalki: Tirthankara Image: Mid 8th Century
   Ambika Image: Early 8th Century
7. Gadi Keshavara: Arhat Parsva: Late 7th Century
8. Kellipusuru: Jinalaya: Mid 7th Century
9. KiruvattekeRe (Karatageri): Santi Bhagavat: AD 600
10. Kisuvolal (Pattadakal): Jinabhavan: AD 560
11. Mallasamudra: Jina Parsva: Circa 7th Century
12. Nandagiri: Jinalaya: AD 750.
13. Pomburca: Bogara Basadi: Early 8th Century
14. PuligeRe: Anesejjeya Basadi 7th Century
    Dhavala Jinalaya: Early 7th Century
    Mokkara Basadi: Early 7th Century
    Sankavasati: Late 6th Century
15. Talakadu: Parsva Image: 7th Century

Alphabetical List of Some Jaina Centres of the Period:

Aduru (Gangi Pandiyur)
Aihole (Ay+hole; Arya Polal)
Annigeri (AnnigeRe): Sk. Anyatataka
Asandilur/Asandyalur (Asandihalli)
Badami (Sk. Vatapi)
Banavasi (Banavase, Vanavasi, Vaijayanatipura)
Bastipura (Kollegala)
Bijavada in Andhra
Gadikesavara: Gulbarga Dt.
Kalvappu (Sk. Katavapura, Sravanabelagola)
KellangeRe
Kellipusur (Kelasuru)
KiruvattekeRe (Karatageri)
Kisuvolal (Sk. Raktapura, Pattadakal, Pattada-Kisuvolal)
Kopananagara (Kopanadri, Koppala)
Mallasamudra (Ballagere)
Narasimharajapura (Simhanagadde)

Palasige (Sk. Palasika, Halasi)
Paraluru (Halluru)
Pomburca (Hombuja/Humca)
Puligere (Laxmesvara)
Punnadu (Punnata)

Annigere (mod. Annigeri), an important town and capital of Belvola-300 district, from Chalukya times, continued to be known as *rājadhāni-paṭṭaṇa*, till the end of Hoysala regime. Annigere, a Kannada place-name, was Sanskritized as Anyatataka, of course, a misnomer.

An inscription, also the earliest record from the place, datable to 751-52, records the construction of Cedia (Sk. Caitya, 'Jaina shrine') by Kaliyamma, headman of Jebulageri, evidently a part of the town of Annigere. The record refers to the 6th regnal year of King Kirtivarma Satyasraya. The pillar on which the epigraph is engraved is at present set up in front of the Banasankari temple, belonged to the Jaina temple. The inscription engraved on three faces of the small pillar further states the erection in front of it of a sculpture by Kondasular Kuppa alias Kirtivarma Gosasi, who, obviously, was Kaliyamma's master.

Mahendravarman I (600–30), the Pallava king, great alike in war and peace, a Jaina before conversion to Saivism, inspired by the Badami cave temples, experimented similar ones at Mandagapattu (South Arcot Dist.), and started the Jaina cave at the celebrated Sittanavasal, which was further embellished by the Pandyas. Architecture of the Aihole caves turned out to be beftting model for the Pallavas, Pandyas and Cholas in Tamil Nadu, and the imperial Rashtrakutas.

Between 7th and 9th centuries, rock-cut caves and huge boulders in the Deccan were targets of skilled sculptors, who were the proteges of royal dynasties mentioned above.

6

Early Chalukya Art and Architecture

S. Rajasekhara

HISTORY

The Early Chalukyas ruled from about AD 535 to AD 757 till they were overthrown by the Rashtrakutas. The Megudi inscription composed by Ravikirti recounts the rule of the Chalukyas till AD 634-35. It refers to Jayasimha and Ranaraga, the grandfather and father respectively of Pulakesi I, the real founder of the Chalukya rule. Inscriptions mention Pulakesi I as a performer of *Asvamedha*-sacrifice. To make his rule strong, he built an impregnable fort at Vatapi in AD 543-44. His son and successor was Kirtivarma I, who expanded the kingdom by defeating the Nalas, the Mauryas and the Kadambas. He is described in an inscription as the *The Maker of Vatapi*. At the time of his death, his son Pulakesi II was still a minor. As such, his younger brother Mangalesa ascended the throne. Mangalesa was a great conqueror and a patron of art and architecture. During his rule, he greatly increased the power and prosperity of the Chalukya family. He defeated the Kalachuris and captured a vast booty. He worshipped Makutesvara at Mahakuta and erected a *Dharmastambha*. His notable achievement in the field of art was the excavation of a cave temple in AD 578 for Vishnu at Badami. Inscriptions call him a *Parama Bhāgavata*. Mangalesa refused to hand over power to Pulakesi II, which resulted in a civil war in which Mangalesa was killed.

Pulakesi II ascended the throne in AD 610. He was the greatest of the Chalukya rulers. The Megudi inscription at Aihole describes at length his military exploits. Soon after his accession, he succeeded in restoring order within the kingdom by putting down the rebellious chiefs. He then started on his military campaigns. He conquered Banavasi, humbled the Mauryas and captured Gharapuri (Elephanta). He subdued the rulers of Lata, Malava and Gujarat. He overran Kosala and Kalinga. He also captured Pishthapura. In the south he clashed with Mahendravarman I of Kanchi and captured the Guntur area. The highlight of Pulakesi II's conquests was his conflict with Harshavardhana, which resulted in the complete discomfiture of the latter's army. As a result of his conquests, the Chalukyas established their sway over the Deccan and parts of south India. However, in AD 642 he was defeated by the Pallava ruler Narasimhavarman I of Kanchi. Vatapi was occupied by the Pallavas for about 13 years. During the rule of Pulakesi II, the Upper and the Lower Sivalayas at Badami and the Megudi at Aiholi were built.

ln AD 655 Vikramaditya I, one of the sons of Pulakesi II, restored the Chalukya rule at Vatapi. Under him, there was a remarkable resurgence of Chalukya power. He defeated three successive Pallava rulers, viz. Narasimhavarman I, Mahendravarman II and Paramesvaravaraman I. A notable event of his rule was his conversion to Saivaism by Sudarsanacharya. He is called in the inscriptions as *Parama Māhēśvara*. The construction of temples which had received a jolt in AD 642 restarted with greater vigour. New centres of art including Alampur emerged in Andhra Pradesh (Fig. 6.16).

Vinayaditya, who ruled between AD 681 and AD 696, undertook an expedition into north India in which his son Vijayaditya distinguished himself as a reputed general by capturing the royal emblems and the *Pāḷidhvaja* from the northern ruler. Under Vinayaditya, the Svarga Bramha temple at Alampur was built in honour of his queen by Lokaditya Ela Arasa. At Ittagi, a *Tōraṇa* was erected. Vijayaditya, who succeeded Vinayaditya and his son Vikramaditya II, were responsible for taking the Chalukya art and architecture to its zenith by their involvement in architectural activities. Vijayaditya continued to fight with the Pallavas. Yuvaraja Vikramaditya invaded the Pallava kingdom and marched as far as Kanchi. Vijayaditya built the first of the Chalukya temples at Pattadakal, when he constructed the present Sangamesvara temple referred to in inscriptions as Vijayesvara temple. In AD 699, Vijayaditya's mother Vinayavati constructed the first Trikuta temple in south India and consecrated in it the images of Bramha, Vishnu and Siva. It is at present known as Jambulinga temple. Vijayaditya's sister, Kumkumamahadevi built a Jaina Basadi at Lakshmesvara and called it Anesajje Basadi.

Vikramaditya II's rule is chiefly noted for the capture of Kanchi around AD 740 and the erection of temples at Pattadakal. To commemorate the capture of Kanchi on three occasions by Vikramaditya II, his two queens, Lokamahadevi and Trailokyesmahadevi built the temples of Lokesvara (Virupaksha) and Trailokyavara (Mallikarjuna) respectively at Pattadakal. An officer of Vikramaditya II by the name Atada Ale Komarasinga built the Durga temple at Aihole. Probably the Mallikarjuna temple at Mahakuta was built during this period.

Kirtivarma II, son and successor of Vikramaditya II, was the last early Chalukya ruler. His rule witnessed the challenges posed by the Rashtrakutas. In AD 757, he was defeated by Rashtrakuta Krishna I. With this defeat, the glorious rule of the Chalukyas came to an end. The period of Kirtivarma II, in spite of military upheavals, witnessed the continuation of architectural activities. A number of temples at Aihole, Badami, Pattadakal and Mahakuta were erected. The best of these temples was the Papanatha temple at Pattadakal.

ARCHITECTURE

Under the early Chalukyas, two distinct types of architecture flourished—the rock-cut architecture and the structural architecture. The rock-cut architecture prevailed between the foundation of the Chalukya rule and its temporary eclipse in AD 642 while structural architecture picked up greater momentum after the restoration of the Chalukya rule in AD 655. All the cave temples are found either at Badami or Aihole while structural temples are found at various places.

Rock-cut Architecture

There are four cave temples at Badami and five at Aihole. Of the caves at Badami, one belongs to the Saivas, two to the Vaishanvas and one to the Jains. The cave temples at Badami share a number of common features like an open courtyard in front of the caves; contain a sanctum, a pillared hall and a veranda; possess a high basement embellished with sculptures of *gaṇas*; the façade marked by a row of four pillars and two pilasters in all the caves except cave III, which has six pillars and two pilasters; separation of the veranda and the pillared hall by a row of pillars with blind bays on the extreme sides; massive pillars which are basically square; the accommodation of *Sankha* and *Padma Nidhis*; flight of steps leading to the sanctum which is excavated at a higher level from that of the pillared hall; the carving of massive sculptures on the walls of the veranda and the decoration of the ceiling of the veranda. There are also traces of paintings in cave II and III.

Cave I is a Saiva cave. Adjacent to the cave, to its left on the front, is a small cell with the sculptures of Ganesa, Kartikeya and Mahishamardini on its walls. Following the Kadamba examples, the Mahishamardini sculpture shows the Devi holding Mahisha by his tail and has been lifted in the air. Outside the cave is the 18-armed Nataraja known for its incomparable composition. The large sculptures in the veranda depict Harihara and Ardhanarisvara. There is also a sculpture of a Dvarapala holding a trident.

Cave II is dedicated to Vishnu. The veranda walls are carved with Varaha and Trivikrama sculptures. The ceiling of the veranda is decorated with the reliefs of Gandharavas, Matsya-Chakra and Vishnu. The entire cave was originally painted in different colours and designs as can be made out from the few traces of paint that can still be seen.

Fig. 6.1. Cave III—Badami.

Cave III is the largest of the cave temples at Badami (Fig. 6.1). According to an inscription in the cave, it was excavated in AD 578 by Mangalesa, younger brother of King Kirtivarma I, to consecrate God Vishnu. Interestingly, another inscription describes the cave temple as Mangalesana Kalmane. It is about seventy feet wide and about fifty feet deep. The basement is in fact built of dressed stones and carved with the figures of Ganas. This cave is chiefly notable for its massive sculptures. At one end of the platform outside the veranda is the huge monumental sculpture of Trivikrama. It is almost eleven feet in height. The eight-armed Trivikrama holding different weapons is in the act of measuring the skies with his left leg. The huge cylindrical-shaped crown is attractive. What stands out in this sculpture is its composition involving many characters like Trivikrama, Vamana, Bali, Sukracharya, Namuchi, Jambavan, Garuda, Chandra and Varuna. The composition is impressive as well as awe-inspiring. Other equally impressive sculptures in the cave are those of Vishnu seated on the coils of Ananta under a five-hooded canopy, Narasimha, Varaha and Harihara. Like the Trivikrama sculpture, the Varaha sculpture, which was once painted, is massive and robust in look proclaiming the unbridled energy of the deity. In the underneath portion of the eave is an impressive Garuda sculpture.

Another set of thirty-three sculptures which draw our attention are the bracket figures placed on the facade pillars. These figures are rather tall and graceful. While some of them depict the love-lorn Nayika, others portray divine couples—Rati and Manmatha, Naga and Nagini and Siva and Parvati. There are yet other bracket figures depiciting Mithunas. These Mithuna figures remind us of the postures mentioned in Vatsayana's *Kāmasūtra.* The bracket figures prepared by different sculptors reflect the aesthetics of the age. These bracket figures became an inspiration for the bracket figures during the subsequent periods, especially under the Hoysalas as can be seen in the Chenna Kesava temple at Belur and the Hoysalesvara temple at Halebid.

In Cave III, the sculptors have made use of the beams in the veranda to chisel miniature narrative sculptures. The narrations are based on epics and Puranas. The themes depicted include *Samudra Manthana, Pārijātāpaharaṇa* and the story of Prahlada. There are also many reliefs depicting the story of Krishna. These narrative sculptures in course of time became a model for the succeeding generations of sculptors, especially during the Hoysala period. These sculptures are very elaborate and detailed in narration.

The underneath portion of the eave of cave III was once covered with painted panels. Unfortunately, these have been obliterated due to ravages of time. At least two of the panels can be identified. One of them, according to C. Sivaramamurti, represents Indra in court enjoying a dance performance. The other is often identified as a scene depicting the Chalukya king Kirtivarma I in court. Another panel depicts a flying Gandharva couple.

Cave IV is a Jaina cave. It is the smallest of the caves at Badami. It was the last of the caves to be excavated at Badami. It was in all probability a cave of Mangalesa's period. Originally, it contained only the image of Jina in the sanctum and the sculptures of Parsvanatha and Bahubali on the walls. However, during the rule of the Chalukyas of Kalyana, a number of large as well as miniature Jina and Yakshi sculptures were carved on the walls of the hall and also on the pillars. A feature noticeable in the sculpture of Bahubali is that he is shown with long hair falling on the shoulders. All the iconographic features of Bahubali were evolved by this time like the anthills with snakes, the *samabhanga* posture of Bahubali, the creepers entwining his arms and legs and the attendants. An important feature which goes largely unnoticed is the presence of counchant lions on whose backs the facade pillars are placed. These pillars with lions for the base later inspired the Pallavas to prepare similar pillars for their temples. They placed the shaft of the pillar on the head of a seated lion. This type of pillar was popular, both in cave and structural architecture, under the Pallavas from the time of Narasimhavarman I.

In between Caves II and III is a natural cavern. In this cavern is a sculpture, which is often identified as a sculpture of Buddha holding a lotus.

While cave temples were being excavated at Badami, similar efforts were also going on at Aihole. The Chalukyas excavated five cave temples at Aihole. Of the five caves, three are larger in size. Of these, the most well known are the Ravanaphadi and the Meen Basadi. The Meena Basadi gets its name from a sculpture carved in the cave wherein a Yaksha holds a fish in his hands. According to some legends, Ravanaphadi is so called because Ravana on his way to Lanka after abducting Sita is said to have rested here. The Buddist chaitya which is the earliest of the caves at Aihole is half-rock cut and half structural in character.

The Buddhist chaitya is half structural and half rock-cut. It is a storied chaitya. The verandas of both the lower and the upper chaitya are structural in character. The chaitya which was once mistaken for a Jina temple has a number of miniature reliefs on the door jambs of the sanctum and the ante-chamber. These reliefs depict incidents from the Jataka stories and the life of the Buddha. Some of these incidents are taken from *Chulla Haṁsa Jātaka,*

Ārāmadūsa Jātaka, Valahassa Jātaka and *Surāpāna Jātaka*. Incidents from the life of the Buddha include the Great Departure, the Nalagiri incident, the First Sermon in the Deer Park at Saranath and the attempt to kill Buddha by Devadatta. The ceiling of the upper veranda has one of the finest sculptures of the period. It shows Buddha in *vyākhyānamudrā*. The upper chaitya once housed a small *stupa* in the sanctum as the semi-circular cut in the rock bed indicates. An image of Buddha, damaged, which was once in the lower chaitya, is now kept in the local museum. It may be noted here that the sanctum door of the upper chaitya has a seated Buddha relief on the lintel. This Buddhist chaitya was the first of the rock-cut edifices at Aihole. It was probably prepared during the rule of Pulakesi I or the beginning of Kirtivarma I's rule.

Meena Basadi was probably excavated in the middle of the 6th century AD. The front wall and the entrance of the cave are structural in character. It has the entire ceiling of the veranda and the inner hall carved with Makaras and floral motifs. This Jaina cave is much earlier in date than the Jain cave at Badami. The most interesting sculptures in the cave are those of Bahubali and Parsvanatha in the veranda and a large panel, unfinished, depicting the three stages in the life of Parsvanatha. This last mentioned panel is admirably planned but surprisingly abandoned by the sculptors. This frieze is interesting more for its composition than for its execution. With the marks of the chisel still deep and bold, the plumb lines still uneffaced, the portions of the face and the body still in the making, the panel has its own appeal and attraction. It satisfies little but evokes more of our curiosity. No panel of such dimension (23 feet in length) appears to have been ever planned on any temple surface by any Karnataka sculptor. The features of Bahubali or Gommata are being standardized in this sculpture. These features include the *samabhanga* posture, the ant hills, the sauntering snakes, the creepers entwining the legs and arms. However, he is shown with long strands of hair falling on his shoulders.

The Ravanaphadi was the last of the cave temples to be excavated during the early Chalukya period. On plan it has a sanctum, an ante-chamber, a hall, and two cells on the two sides of the hall. In front of the cave is the Nandi platform and behind it is a tall pillar much like the Mahakuta pillar. In the Ravanaphadi, the sidewalls of the ante-chamber have large sculptures of Varaha and Mahishamardhini. The fact that in the Varaha sculpture, Bhudevi sits on the left shoulder of Varaha indicates that the cave was probably excavated in the beginning of the seventh century. The cell on the right side has a ten-armed Nataraja in a graceful dancing posture. His dance is witnessed by the Saptamatrikas, Parvati, Ganesh, Kartikeya, Nandi and Bhringi.

STRUCTURAL ARCHITECTURE

The structural temples of the early Chalukyas are concentrated at five places, viz. Aihole, Badami, Mahakuta and Pattadakal in Karnataka and Alampur in Andhra Pradesh. There are also a number of other places where temples of the early Chalukyas are found. These include Sulebhavi, Bhadranayakana Jalihal, Huligemmana Kolla, Naganatha Kolla, Siddhana Kolla, Hunagund, Itagi, Banavasi and Kumaraswami Hill near Sandur in Karnataka and at Satyavolu, Kudaveli Sangama (now shifted to Alampur), Kadamara Kalava, Mahanandi and Panyam in Andhra Pradesh. Like the history of the Chalyukyas, the development of structural architecture too falls under two phases, viz. those that were built before AD 642 and those built after AD 655.

The temples of Upper Sivalaya and the Lower Sivalaya at Badami, the small Dravida temple near Ravanaphadi (Fig. 6.3) and the Megudi at Aihole, and the Mahakutesvara and the Banantigudi at Mahakuta (Fig. 6.2) are the earliest of the Chalukya temples. All these temples are in Dravida style. Of the four Chalukya centres in Karnataka, it was

Fig. 6.2. Bananti Gudi, Mahakuta.

Fig. 6.3. Temple near Ravanaphadi, Aihole.

at Aihole that many experiments were made in the construction of temples on different plans (Fig. 6.5) and in different architectural styles. We come across both Dravida and Rekha Nagara temples in this place. In addition, temples with Kadamba Nagara *śikhara* were also erected. There are also temples without any superstructure. The temples of Durga, Chakragudi, Huchachappayyangudi and Huchchimalligudi can be mentioned as examples for Rekha Nagara temples. The Mallikarjuna and Galaganatha can be cited as examples for Kadamba Nagara style. What is of importance is that at Aihole, as noted above, different temple plans were adopted. We come across *sāndhāra* and *nirandhāra* temples, i.e. respectively with or without circumambulatory passage. There are temples on *gajapṛishṭha* or apsidal plan. There are two apsidal temples at Aihole. The most famous of these is the Durga temple built during the rule of Vikramaditya II and dedicated to God Surya. There are temples with the sanctum built against the back wall of the pillared hall. These are often called *Manṭapa* type of temples. The Lad Khan and the Kontgudi can be noted as examples for this. In the architecture of the Jains, the Megudi occupies a very significant place. Here, in addition to the main sanctum, an additional sanctum was built above the roof of the lower sanctum. Building storied Basadis gained popularity in course of time under the Rashtrakutas,

Fig. 6.4. Apsidal Siva temple, Hale Mahakuta.

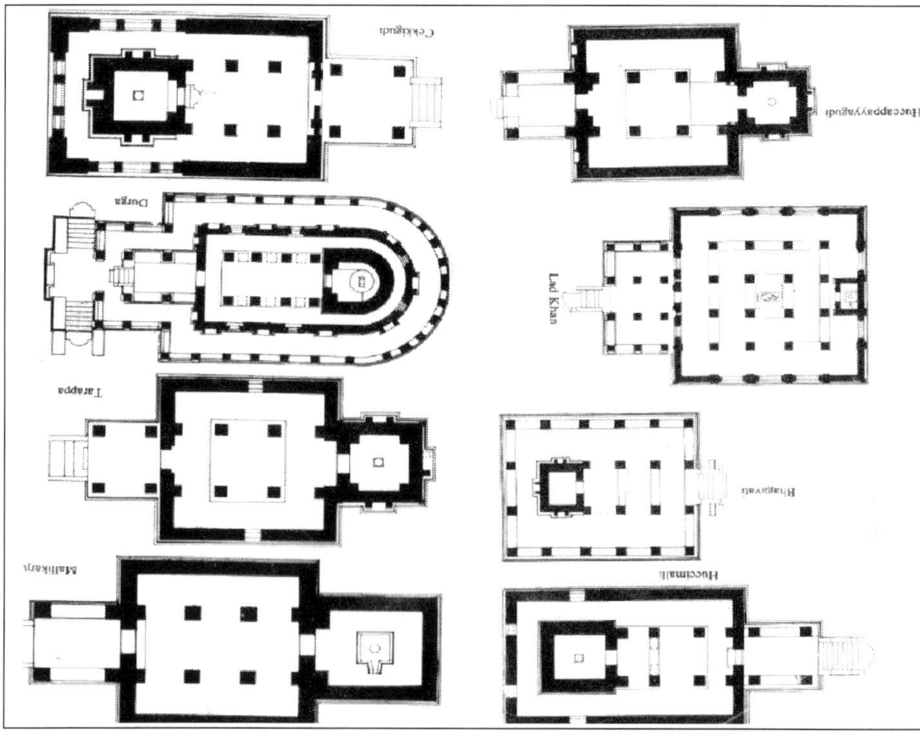

Fig. 6.5. Temple plans, Aihole.

Chalukyas of Kalyana and the Gangas. At Lakkundi, the Brahma Jinalaya built by Attimabbe is a storied basadi. Perhaps the best known example of a storied basadi is the Chavundaraya Basadi at Sravana Belagola.

The temples at Aihole that need to be noted are the Megudi built in AD 634-35 by Ravikirti to consecrate Jinedra (who may be Neminatha), the Huchchmalligudi built in the beginning of the 7th century AD noted for its unpretentious *Rekha Nagara śikhara* lacking in curves, the Huchachappayyanagudi in *Rekha Nagara* order built by the architect Narasobba, which is noted for some of the finest miniature Gana sculptures on its beams, the Lad Khan temple on which a lot has been written, and the Durga temple as grand a temple as the Virupaksha temple at Pattadakal.

The only temple which has a foundation inscription mentioning the date of the temple and the name of the builder

Fig. 6.6. Bhutanatha temple, Badami.

is the Megudi at Aihole. Located on top of a hill this temple, which is in fact a basadi was built by Ravikirti, a poet who lived in the court of Pulakesi II. It was constructed in AD 634-35. The well-known Aihole *Praśasti* composed by Ravikirti is found engraved on the wall of this basadi. The basadi built on a high basement comprises of a sanctum, an *antarāḷa*, a *pradakshiṇāpatha*, a *navaranga*, an *ardhamanṭapa* and a pillared porch. At a later date, an upper sanctum with a porch (now completely missing) was added. The sanctum has on its back wall the sculpture of a Jina. In the *antarāḷa* was once kept a large sculpture of Ambika, now shifted to the local museum. This sculpture is a marvellous piece of work, unsurpassed in beauty and elegance by any other Ambika sculptures in India. The workmanship is bold and the plastic content of the sculpture is unrivalled. Whether the presence of Ambika, also known as Kushmandini, indicates that the basadi was meant to consecrate Neminatha is anybody's guess. Ambika is the *yakshi* of Neminatha.

The Durga temple (Fig. 6.8) is a temple built for Aditya or Sun god. It is built on *gajaprishṭha* plan. It is the largest structural temple to be built on apsidal plan in the whole of south India. It consists of an apsidal sanctum, an apsidal closed

Fig. 6.7. Lad Khan temple, Aihole.

pradakshiṇāpatha, a *sabhāmanṭapa* which is adjoined by a *mukhamanṭapa* and surrounding all these sections of the temple is a half-open outer *pradakshiṇāpatha*. Above the sanctum rises a *Rekha Nagara śikhara*, a part of which has fallen. The huge *āmalaka*, which once stood on top of the *śikhara* is lying on the ground nearby. The outer walls fitted with a large number of niches and windows contain large-sized sculptures. These include Harihara, Vishnu riding Garuda, Siva standing against Nandi, Mahishamardini, Varaha, Harihara and Narasimha (Figs. 6.9 and 6.10). Another sculpture which once belonged to a niche in the Durga temple is that of Bhikshatana Siva, now kept in the local museum. The large pillar sculptures of the *mukhamanṭapa* depict in addition to deities, *Rasika Dampatis* in postures like *Latāvēshṭhika-Alingana* based on Vatsayana's *Kāmasūtra* (Fig. 6.11). An added feature of the Durga temple is an entrance *manṭapa* on the right side of the temple. An inscription engraved on the wall of this *manṭapa* refers to a gift to God Aditya. An inscription engraved on the side of the steps leading to the temple refers to Atada Ale

Fig. 6.8. Durga temple, Aihole.

Komarasinga, who built this temple. As the temple shares a number features found in the Virupaksha and Mallikarjuna temples at Pattadakal and the presence of Vikramditya's inscriptions gives credence to it being placed as a temple of Vikramaditya II's period.

Fig. 6.9. Siva, Durga temple, Aihole.

The Lad Khan (Fig. 6.7), on which much has been written, is a structure which belongs to either the close of the 7th century AD or the beginning of the 8th century AD. Earlier scholars like Henry Cousens have placed it in AD 450. This temple shares a number of features found in the Jambulinga temple at Badami built in AD 699 by Vinayavati, mother of Vijayaditya. The Lad Khan consists of a large square pillared hall with a sanctum built

Fig. 6.10. Mahishamardini, Durga temple, Aihole.

Fig. 6.11. Latavestitika Alingana sculpture, Durga temple, Aihole.

against the back wall of this hall. Adjoining the pillared hall is a *mukhamanṭapa*. The pillars in the hall are square in shape with *taranga* brackets. There are large stone grilles on the side walls. The back wall has small windows. One of them is of *matsya-chakra* design. The sanctum was built against the back wall at a later date. The upper storey of the Lad Khan is also a later addition. The *mukhamanṭapa* has square pillars, which are richly carved. Some of the pillars have large-sized sculptures of Ganga, Yamuna, Kinnaras and amorous couples. Two of the pillars are carved with the royal insignia of Varaha and the umbrella with whisks. The Lad Khan was originally the headquarters of the Ayyavole Guild. The patron deity of the guild was Durga Bhagavati. Close by is a temple for Durga Bhagavati, now locally called Goudaragudi. It has a square open-pillared hall with a sanctum built in the middle of it. The hall also acts as an open *pradakshiṇā*. A notable feature of the temple is its exquisitely carved sanctum door. The lintel has a Garuda while in the architrave, a gracefully carved Gajalakshmi can be seen.

Fig. 6.12. Huchchimalli Gudi, Aihole.

The Huchchimalligudi (Fig. 6.12) is a temple that originated at the beginning of the 7th century. It is a temple of medium proportions. Built on a high basement it consists of a sanctum, a *pradakshiṇāpatha,* a *sabhāmanṭapa* and a square *mukhamanṭapa*. Some scholars have described this temple as a temple where for the first time *antarāḷa* is introduced. This is based on the presence of a screened doorway in between two pillars in the *sabhāmanṭapa* in front of the sanctum. In reality this is not an early Chalukya creation but a doorframe of the Vijayanagara times. There is no such thing as an *antarāḷa* in this temple. The Huchchimalli has small square stone windows on the outer walls to light the *pradakshiṇāpatha*. This Siva temple once had a multi-armed dancing sculpture of Siva. It is now kept in the local museum. An interesting aspect of the temple is its *Rekha Nagara śikhara*. The curves of the *śikhara* are not at all prominent. In fact, it looks like a straight line. The *śukanāsa* contains a large sculpture of Dancing Siva in its *chaitya*. The Huchchimalligudi is most propbaly the earliest temple with a *Rekha Nagara śikhara*. On the ceiling of the *mukhamanṭapa* is a finely carved sculpture of Kartikeya in the act of slaying Tarakasura with a spear.

The Huchchappayyagudi (Fig. 6.13) located near the bank of the Malaprabha River is a temple with a *Rekha Nagara śikhara*. It is a small temple with only a sanctum, a *sabhāmanṭapa* and a square *mukhamanṭapa* on the front. This is the only temple at Aihole about whose architect we have some information. An inscription in the *mukhamanṭapa* eulogises Narasobba as a great architect, the like of which was not born before nor would one be born in future. At Aihole itself, there is another inscription on a boulder near the Meena Basadi, which eulogises Narasobba. Incidentally here, on the boulder, we come across a sketch of what

Fig. 6.13. Huchchappayyana Gudi, Aihole.

would have been the facade of a cave. The plumb lines are still fresh. Why it was not finished is not known. The beams in the *sabhāmanṭapa* are carved with very beautifully chiselled figures of *gaṇas* in various postures. Above the *sabhāmanṭapa* door, on the inside, is a large panel of Gajalakshmi. On the outside, the niches on the walls of the sanctum contain large sculptures of Narasimha and Gajasurasamharamurti. At the entrance into the *mukhamanṭapa* are carved Śankha and Padma Nidhis. The pillars of the *mukhamanṭapa* have large sculptures on the shafts depicting Kinnaras. Incidentally, some of the sculptures in the temple were the works of Ganasobba, who is mentioned as a sculptor in an inscription in the temple. Whether Ganasobba was a son of Narasobba is anybody's guess. The temple, which has quite a number of features of temples built in the 8th century, can be placed in the first half of the 8th century.

We may note here a few more temples of the 8th century with *Rekha Nagara śikhara*. These include Chakragudi and

Fig. 6.14. Huchchappayyana matha, Aihole.

Tarappagudi. The latter displays square dentil heads on top of the basement just below the niches which are built on the walls. These dentil heads remind us of similar dentils in the Galaganatha temple at Pattadakal and in the temples at Alampur.

Another temple worth noting is the Huchchappayya Matha (Fig. 6.14). This temple does not possess any superstructure above the sanctum. The temple is of the *Manṭapa* variety. This temple is chiefly noted for the excellent ceiling sculptures of the Trimurtis. The sculpture of Siva is dynamic in composition. The temples in the Kontgudi group are also of *Manṭapa* type. By the side of the Huchchappayya Matha is a secular structure belonging to the post early Chalukya period.

Among the temples that have Kadamba Nagara and its variant *śikhara,* one can note the temples of Mallikarjuna and Galaganatha. The Galaganatha temple is located near the Malaprabha river. The group of temples near the river include both early Chalukya and Rashtrakuta temples.

Fig. 6.15. Naganatha temple, Naganathana Kolla.

Badami, right from the establishment of the Chalukya rule, enjoyed patronage from the royalty and the rich people when it came to beautifying the capital city. The well-known temples at Badami are at present known as Upper Sivalaya, Lower Sivalaya, Malegitti Sivalaya, and Jambulinga temples. The Bhutanatha temple built on the edge of the Agastya tank leaves a visitor spellbound because of its scenic beauty. The Upper and Lower Sivalayas were built before AD 642. The Upper Sivalaya has many features, which are to be seen in the Megudi at Aihole. The Malegatti Sivalaya was probably built when Vikramaditya I was the ruler. An inscription on the temple wall mentions that the architect of the temple was Aryaminchi Upadhyaya. It is a temple located on the edge of a cliff and is of the Dravida order. The Jambulinga was built in AD 699 by Vinayavati, mother of Vijayaditya. The Bhutanatha temple is a structure built in the closing years of the early Chalukya period. The Upper Sivalaya was originally a Vishnu temple as indicated by the three sculptures of Kalingamardana

Fig. 6.16. Rekha Nagara temple at Alampur.

Krishna, Narasimha and Govardhanagiridhari Krishna on the outer walls of the temple. The *Dravida śikhara* has no *śukanāsa.* There are narrative sculptures in the basement. The Jambulinga is the first *trikūṭa* temple of the structural variety in south India. An inscription in the temple states that in it were installed Bramha, Vishnu and Siva. On plan it has three sanctums facing three different directions, a large pillared hall and a *mukhamanṭapa.* This *trikūṭa* temple became a model for the subsequent *trikūṭas* built in Karnataka. At Aihole we have a few *trikūṭas* built during the Rashtrakuta period. For example, the Kundargi group of temples.

From the beginning of the 8th century AD, Pattadakal, called Pattada Kisuvolal in inscriptions, gained in prominence and emerged as the greatest centre of Chalukya art. The earliest of the temples here was built by Vijayaditya. An inscription refers to the present Sangamesvara temple as Vijayesvara temple. Unfortunately, the temple was left incomplete. However, in this temple a few new features were introduced in Chalukya architecture like erecting separate shrines for Mahishamardini and Ganapati in the pillared

Fig. 6.17. Sangmesvara temple, Pattadakal.

hall on either side of the sanctum. This temple has a pure form of *Dravida śikhara* without the *śukanāsa* or the projection on the front of the *śikhara*. The *śukanāsa* is a very conspicuous feature of *Rekha Nagara śikhara*. The other five temples of significance at Pattadakal are the Galaganatha, Papanatha, Kadasiddhesvara, Jambunatha (Fig. 6.24) Virupaksha and Mallikarjuna. The latter two were constructed by the two queens of Vikramaditya II. The elder queen, Lokamahadevi, built the Lokesvara (Virupaksha) to commemorate the conquest of Kanchi on three occasions by Vikramaditya II. Her uterine sister Trailokyamahadevi built the Trailokyesvara (Mallikarjuna) temple. These two temples possess *Dravida śikharas* with *śukanāsa*, a feature not found in the pure form of *Dravida śikhara*.

Among the early Chalukya temples of the 8th century, the Virupaksha temple at Pattadakal is a landmark in the architectural history of Karnataka (Fig. 6.20). Built on the bank of the

Fig. 6.18. Side view, Sangamesvara temple, Pattadakal.

Malaprabha River by Lokamahadevi, the senior queen of Vikramaditya II, to commemorate the conquest of Kanchi on three occasions by the Chalukya king, the Virupaksha temple complex represents the finest architectural creation of the early

Fig. 6.19. Galaganath temple, Pattadakal.

Fig. 6.20. Virupaksha temple, Pattadakal.

Chalukya period. It is a *sāndhāra* temple built in Dravida style. It is also the largest and the most elaborately embellished among the early Chalukya temples. It stands within a large courtyard surrounded by Parivara shrines along the *prākāra* walls and entered through large gateways on the east and the west. The temple consists of a *garbhagṛiha*, a *pradakshiṇāpatha*, a *sabhāmanṭapa* with two small shrines for Mahishamardini and Ganesha in it. The *sabhāmanṭapa* opens into three small porches. In front of the temple stands a large square *Nandimanṭapa*.

The temple stands on a high basement. The outer walls are decorated with pilasters, *kōshṭhas* and large sculptures and beautifully chiselled *jālandhras*. The *jālandhras* are of different designs like geometrical patterns, birds, etc. The *kōshṭhas* contain large sculptures with a few of them mentioning the name of the sculptor who carved them. One such beautifully carved sculpture is that of Siva standing in *tribhanga* on Apasmara with his *jaṭas* spread on either side of his head (Fig. 6.22). This sculpture was carved by Changamma. Other sculptures that need to be noted are those of Lingodbhava Siva (Fig. 6.21), Ravana fighting with Jatayu, Siva killing Andhakasura, Lakaulisa, Nataraja, Siva and Parvati, Ardhanarisvara and Vishnu. A feature of the Virupaksha temple are the large pillar sculptures in the three porches. These

Fig. 6.21. Lingodhbhava Siva, Virupaksha temple, Pattadakal.

Fig. 6.22. Siva, Virupaksha temple, Pattadakal.

sculptures include *dvārapālas*, Ravana trying to lift Mount Kailasa, Gajendramoksha, etc. Such pillar sculptures first appear in the Naganatha temple at Naganathakolla (Fig. 6.15). The ceiling sculptures of the three porches also contain sculptures of great beauty.

The *garbhagṛiha dvāra* is marked by a beautifully sculpted *makara tōraṇa* just above the lintel, which has a relief of Siva and Parvati riding Nandi. The doorframe is further decorated with Saiva *dvārapālas*. The *pradakshiṇāpatha* is sufficiently wide and is fitted with 6 stone grilles—two on each of the walls. It is the *sabhāmanṭapa* that attracts our attention. The large *sabhāmanṭapa* has massive looking pillars supporting the ceiling. There are 18 pillars in four rows. These pillars are square with a *patta* in the upper part of the shaft, which is decorated with small reliefs. These reliefs are narrative in nature. The narrative sculptures represent incidents from the *Mahābhārata*, *Samudramanthana* or the Churning of the Ocean, the *Gaṅgāvataraṇa* or the Decent of the river goddess Ganga and *Yaśōdhara Charita*. The medallion decorations on the pillars portray in some instances incidents from the *Pañchatantra*. The ceiling of the central nave is high. They once contained the sculptures of the *Trimurtis*. In addition, there is a fine sculpture of coiled Nagaraja with five hoods above the head. The *sabhāmanṭapa* has twelve stone grilles so that it gets sufficient light. The three porches contain large sculptures on the shaft of the pillars. Some of these sculptures represent *dvārapālas*, Ravana trying to lift Mount Kailasa, Vishnu rescuing Gajendra and Rasika Dampatis.

Opposite the temple is a large square *Nandimanṭapa* measuring 25 feet by 25 feet. There are a number of sculptures, small in size, of Rasika Dampatis. The present Nandi found in the temple is later in date. The original red sandstone Nandi is now found outside the *prākāra* entrance on the east.

There are a number of inscriptions in the temple and its premises. Some of them refer to architects. The inscriptions referring to Sarvasiddhi Achari together with the records referring to the conquest of Kanchi and the visit of Vikramaditya II to the Rajasimhesvara (Kailasanatha) temple in the Pallava capital city, have all led to the foundation of a very widely accepted opinion among historians. They believe that the Virupaksha temple at Pattadakal was inspired by the Pallava art traditions and was built by Pallava artisans.

In 1926, in his description of the Virupaksha temple, Henry Cousens wrote, "Within the temple of Rajasimhesvara at Canjeevaram is an inscription of Vikramaditya which records that Vikramaditya Satyasraya did not confiscate the property of that temple but returned it to the god." The Vokkaleri copperplate grant of his son Kirtivarma II tells us that after his conquest of Kanchi, King Vikramaditya was so impressed by the images and the sculptures in the Rajasimhesvara temple that he not only made gifts to the god but also had the images overlaid with gold. It seems likely that Vikramaditya was so struck with the Kanchi temples that he induced some of the best architects of that place to accompany him to Badami. This surmise receives some support from the two inscriptions incised on the gateway of the Virupaksha temple. One of them speaks of the builder of Lokesvara

(Virupaksha) temple as "the most eminent Sutradhari of the southern country". Henry Cousens further writes, "High upon the front or east face of the temple of Papanatha at Pattadakal is an inscription in praise of a certain Chatta Revadi Ovajja who is said to have "made the southern country", that is, was the builder of the temples in the southern country and hence, by inference, the builder of this one. He belonged to the same guild to which Sarvasiddhi Achari, the builder of Virupaksha belonged.

Benjamin Rowland almost echoes what Henry Cousens had said of these architects. He says, "Vikramaditya persuaded architects and workers from Kanchi to return with him to Pattadakal." He further writes, "An inscription in the Virupaksha temple seems to confirm this, since it speaks of the shrines having been built by the most eminent *sūtradhāri* of the southern country. It is of the typically Dravidian type, with a series of terraced roofs above the sanctuary, dominated by the characteristic *stūpika* of the Dravidian order." Referring to the Virupaksha temple, Ananda K. Coomaraswamy writes:

> The most important of the temples at Pattadakal dates from the first half of the eighth century and shows the strongest possible evidences of Pallava influence. The great Virupaksha temple . . . was most likely built by workmen brought from Kanchipuram and is a direct imitation of the Kailasanath of Kanchipuram where an inscription of Vikramaditya engraved at the time of his conquest, *c.* 740, is to be found.

This opinion that the Pallava artists were involved in the construction of the Virupaksha has been repeated by a large number of scholars.

It was Percy Brown who for the first time raised doubts regarding the employment of workmen from Kanchi in the construction of the Virupaksha temple when he wrote, "there is in these temples, no contribution from the Dravidian style that was not already in regular use in the Chalukya country". He also speaks of close contact between the two regions, namely Karnataka and Tamil Nadu.

It is a historical fact that there were close contacts and also frequent clashes between the early Chalukyas and the Pallavas from the time of Pulakesi II. These contacts did result in exchange of ideas and art traditions between the peoples of the two regions. When Vikramaditya II captured Kanchi for the third time, he had with him Mahasandhivigrahi Anivarita Punyavallabha, who was also a composer-scribe. Anivarita was responsible for the engraving of the inscription of Vikramaditya II in the Rajasimhesvara temple. Like the king, he too must have been impressed by the beauty of the temple and carried back to Badami his impression of the artistic beauty of the temple. When Queen Lokamahadevi desired to build a temple to commemorate the king's conquest of Kanchi, Vikramaditya envisaged a temple of great proportions and artistic excellence to rival the one he had seen at Kanchi. He entrusted the construction of the temple to the leading architects and sculptors of his kingdom, who were adept in building a temple in the Dravidian style.

Pallava traditions, as seen in the Virupaksha temple, are confined to just two instances—a sculptural theme related to Durga and the shrines for the attendant deities. Just this fact does not make Sarvasiddhi Achari a Pallava architect. Moreover, the temple is not a replica of the Kailasanatha temple at Kanchi.

At this juncture, let us note what the inscriptions in the Virupaksha temple speak of. Three of the inscriptions mention architects. An inscription on a pillar at the entrance to the *prākāra* reads: *Svasti Vikramāditya –Śrī- Pṛithivī-vallabha Mahadēviyara Dēgulamān maḍida sūtradhāri Śrī- Guṇḍan Anivāritāchārige mūme perjjeṛepu pattamu Tribhuvanachari yendu pesar-ittu prasādaṅ-geydār...*

It states that Gunda Anivaritachari, the architect of the temple, which was constructed by the queen (Mahadevi) of Vikramaditya, was honoured with *perjjeṛepu* ceremony thrice and was bestowed the title of *Tribhuvanāchāri.*

The second inscription on a pilaster in the porch at the entrance into the *prākāra* reads:

Svasti Śrī –Vikramāditya- bhaṭārar-mmūme Kaṃchiyān-mūme parājisidorā Śrī- Lōkamahādēviyarā ī Lōkēśvara māḍida sūtradhārige mūme- perjjeṛpu geyda -baḷikke ī viṣayadā vinnāṇigalā baḷḷi-gavarettiyān-uḷipida āchāriya pesar-ivan-aṛimi Svasti Śrī- Sarvasiddhi Āchāri sakala guṇ-āśraya-anēkara(ūe)pu- vāstu-Pitamahan sakala-niṣkala- sūkṣhm-āti-bhāṣitan vāstu- prāsāda –yān-āsana- sayana -maṇi mukuṭa ratna-chūḍa-mani teṃkaṇa diśeyā sūtradhāri

It refers to Vikramaditya's conquest of Kanchi thrice and that the architect of the temple of Lokesvara, built by Queen Lokamahadevi, was honoured thrice with the *perjjeripu* ceremony. It also records that the architect, Sarvasiddhi Achari, was proficient in building temples, in preparing sculptures and was an adept in *yōgāsana* and that he was the builder of the southern portion of the temple.

The third inscription engraved on the *Nandimanṭapa* simply states that Sarvasiddhi Acharyi was the architect of the southern portion of the temple. It reads: *Śrī Sarvasiddhi Ācharya teṁkaṇa diśeya sūtradhāri.*

It is clear from the above three inscriptions that the Virupaksha temple was built under the supervision of two architects and not one as commonly believed. They were Gunda Anivaritachari and Sarvasiddhi Achari. They seem to have divided the work of supervision of the construction of the temple. Sarvasiddhi Achari supervised the construction of the southern portion of the temple and Gunda Anivaritachari supervised the construction of the northern portion of the temple. The words *teṇkaṇa diśeyā sūtradhāri* used to describe Sarvasiddhi Achari in the inscriptions simply mean that he was in charge of building the southern portion of the temple and that it does not mean that he was an architect from the southern country (taken to mean Pallava kingdom). That *teṃkaṇa diśe* does not mean southern country, which is made clear by an inscription found in the Papanatha temple at Pattadakal itself. It reads:

Svasti Śrī –Śilemuddara marman Sarvasiddhi Āchārjjyara chaṭṭar Rēvaḍi Ovajjar teṃkaṇa- diśe māḍidōr.

According to this inscription, Revadi Ovajja, grandson of Silemudda and disciple of Sarvasiddhi Acharya, constructed the southern portion of the temple. He is referred to as *tenkaṇa diśe māḍidōr,* meaning one who built the southern portion (of the temple). Hence, *tenkaṇa diśe* should be interpreted to mean "southern part or side" and not southern country or Pallava region. An interesting feature to note is that Revadi Ovajja, the architect, was involved in the construction of a *rekha nagara* temple. It may be noted here that Papanatha temple was a *rekha nagara* temple. If Sarvasiddhi Acharya was from the Pallava territory, then it is very difficult to believe that he was *guru* to a disciple, who built a *rekha nagara* temple. If he was a Pallava architect, he could not have trained anyone in a style with which the Pallava architects and artists were not at all familiar. Further, there is not a single *rekha nagara* temple built during the Pallava period.

In the Badami-Aihole-Pattadakal-Mashakuta region, the architects were familiar with both the Dravida and Nagara architectural traditions. Obviously, Sarvasiddhi Acharya was a Chalukya architect trained in both the architectural styles. He could supervise the southern portion of the Virupaksha temple, which was Dravida in style but at the same time had trained disciples like Revadi Ovajja in northern style of architecture.

It is generally believed that the architects of Pallava territory developed the Dravida style of architecture and that this style originated in the Pallava kingdom. Further, there is the belief that the architects of Karnataka borrowed this style from the Pallavas. Even this presumption that Dravida style originated in Pallava kingdom is not based on any sound evidences.

The Dravida architectural style originated and prospered during the early Chalukya period in the Badami-Aihole-Mahakuta region. The earliest Dravidian temples of the Pallavas are the monolithic *rathas* and the Shore temple at Mahabalipuram executed during the rule of Narasimhavarman I, after his return from Badami in AD 642. However, the early Chalukya architects had developed the Dravidian style almost a century earlier. For example, one can see the complete models of *kūṭa* and *śāla* temples sculpted above the sanctum door in the III Cave temple (AD 578) at Badami. Similar models of *śāla* and *kūṭa* temples are also seen above the sanctum door in the upper floor of the Buddhist chaitya at Aihole. Such decorative carvings were later translated into actual temples for the first time by the early Chalukyas. The earliest such examples of Dravidian temples are the Banantigudi at Mahakuta and a small Dravida temple near the Ravanaphadi cave at Aihole. By AD 635, the early Chalukya architects had already built many temples in Dravida style, such as the Upper Sivalaya and the Lower Sivalaya at Badami, the Makutesvara at Mahakuta and the

Megudi at Aihole. Some of them have *śikharas* in pure Dravida style, i.e. they do not have any projection in the front portion of the *śikhara*. All of them have *stūpis*. The Upper Sivalaya has a square *stūpi* while the Lower Sivalaya has an octagonal *stūpi*.

At Pattadakal itself, there is the Vijayesvara (Sangamesvara) (Figs. 6.17 & 6.18) temple hardly 100 m away from the Virupaksha temple. The Sangamesvara temple was built by Vijayaditya at the beginning of the 8th century. This temple in Dravida style has a pure Dravida *śikhara* without any projection or *śukanāsa* in the front of the *śikhara*. It may be noted here that the temples of Virupaksha and Mallikarjuna have a *śukanāsa* in the *śikhara*. During the beginning of Vikramaditya I's rule, after the restoration of the early Chalukya rule, attempts to blend a *śukanāsa* which is purely a conspicuous feature of *Rekha Nagara śikhara*, into a Dravida *śikhara* were made. This was first attempted in the small temple of Taraka Brahma at Alampur. This little temple seems to have influenced the architects of the Virupaksha and the Mallikarjuna temples to accommodate the *śukanāsa* in the *śikhara*. It may be noted here that in the Pallava temples, the *śikhara* does not contain a *śukanāsa*. It is therefore obvious that the temples of Virupaksha and Mallikarjuna were constructed by the early Chalukya architects and that these temples were not the creations of any Pallava architects.

The Mallikrajuna temple is almost a replica of the Virupaksha temple with its large-sized sculptures on the walls, the narrative sculptures on the pillars, separate shrines for *Parivar Devatas* and the two entrances into its courtyard. Probably, the sculptors who worked in the Virupaksha temple were involved in the construction and beautification of the temple (Figs. 6.25 & 6.23).

The Galaganatha temple, though damaged to a great extent, still retains great charm (Fig. 6.19 & 6.23). The *Rekha Nagara śikhara* is very impressive in spite of the face that the entire *śukanāsa* is missing. The basement in certain sections has square dentil heads which remind us of similar dentils present in the temples at Alampur. The accommodation of blind porches on the outer walls is a novel feature introduced for the first time at Pattadakal. These blind porches contain stone grilles and large sculptures. One such sculpture which can be seen even now is that

Fig. 6.23. View of Galagantha and Mallikarjuna temples, Pattadakal.

of Siva killing Andhakasura. The Kasivisvesvara temple of smaller dimensions is nevertheless of importance because of its unique *śikhara*. Here the *chaitya* motifs are so designed that they look like *jalis*. The pillars inside the temple possess friezes portraying the sculptures of Gajasurasamhara Siva, Ravana trying to lift Mount Kailasa, Lingodhbhava Siva, Tripurasamhari Siva and the *Balalilas* of Krishna.

The Papanatha temple with *Rekha Nagara śikhara* was originally a small temple but was subsequently enlarged. This was the last of the great temples to be built during the early Chalukya rule. An inscription in the temple refers to Revadi Ovajja as the architect of the southern portion of the temple. Following the example of the Galaganatha temple in the same place, the Papanatha too has porches which are blind. These porches are fitted with grilles and large-sized sculptures. However, the main feature of this temple is the treatment of the outer walls. The entire outer wall is carved with narrative sculptures. These sculptures depict various incidents from the *Ramayana.* These incidents are vividly portrayed. A point of interest is that the names of the characters depicted in the scenes are incised so that the viewer

Fig. 6.24. Jambhunath temple, Pattadakal.

understands the sculptured panels. Baladeva and Chengamma, who were associated with the Virupaksha temple, were employed to carve a few sculptures in this temple. A work of Baladeva which fully reveals his artistic skills is the Nataraja panel on the ceiling of the porch. This autographed panel shows a ten-armed Siva dancing to the beat of the cymbals and the *ghaṭa,* while Parvati, standing on a lotus, solemnly watches it. Another masterpiece of Baladeva is the *aṣṭha-dikpālaka* panel found on the ceiling of the central hall. This is more elaborately carved than the Nataraja panel in the porch. In the centre is an exquisitely chiselled Naga sculpture. This Naga sculpture is as good a piece of art as that of the Naga panel in the porch of the Durga temple at Aihole. Around it are the eight guardians. Here, Baladeva calls himself as *bhayaduran* ("devoid of fear"). In the same hall, he carved another Nataraja sculpture. Baladeva was a specialist in carving *dvārapāla* sculptures. In the Papanatha temple, he carved the *dvārapāla* image in the eastern *ardhamanṭapa.* It is autographed by him. Unfortunately, the sculpture is damaged. Baladeva also worked on some of the narrative reliefs on the outer wall of the Papanatha temple. A panel showing Lakshmana cutting off the nose of Surpanakha is autographed by him.

Mahakuta was a well-known Saiva pilgrimage centre even before the early Chalukyas appeared on the political map of south India. The Mahakuta inscription of Mangalesa refers to a gift given to God Makutesvara. The temples at Mahakuta are built around Vishnu Pushkarani. Here as at Pattadakal, we can see temples built in different styles. The two large temples of Mahakutesvara and Mallikarjuna are of Dravida order while others are either of Rekha Nagara order or Kadamba Nagara order. Outside the complex,

Fig. 6.25. Mallikarjuna temple, Pattadakal.

there are two hillocks. On the small hillock outside the temple complex is a small temple locally called Banantigudi. Built in Dravida style, this temple happens to be one of the earliest Dravida temples of the early Chalukya period. It was probably built in the middle of the 6th century AD. The other temple built on the hillock behind the temple complex is identified by some scholars with the Makutesvara temple of Mangalesa's pillar inscription. It is in fact a structure of the 8th century AD. What is interesting is that it is not a temple at all. It is just a pillared hall meant for resting. The present Mahakutesvara temple is a structure which seems to have replaced an earlier dilapidated temple. The present structure was probably built during the closing years of either Vinayaditya or in the first few years of Vijayaditya's rule. This temple has a pure form of Dravida *śikhara* with an octagonal *stūpi*. The basement is carved with narrative sculptures and the most famous of them depicts the *Bhū-Kailāsa* episode. The outer walls of the temple are fitted with stone grilles of different designs. The Mallikarjuna temple, built

Fig. 6.26. Memorial temple for Vikramaditya-II, Huligemmana Kolla.

during the reign of Vikramaditya II, is noted for the large sculptures on its walls and for the stone grilles of different designs. There are also some beautiful *gaṇa* sculptures in the basement. The small Rekha Nagara and Kadamba Nagara temples are chiefly noted for their fine sculptures set in niches on the walls. Some of these represent Narasimha, Harihara, Ardhanarisvara and Lakulisa. There are a large number of Lakulisa sculptures indicating the large following that Lakulisa had at Mahakuta.

Hale Mahakuta is chiefly known for its apsidal temple for Siva (Fig. 6.4). Located on the edge of a tank, this apsidal temple of modest proportions consists of a sanctum which is apsidal, a narrow apsidal circumambulatory passage, a pillared hall and probably a porch which is now completely missing. This is the earliest apsidal temple of the early Chalukya period. This temple inspired the other apsidal temples built at Aihole. It had a *Rekha Nagara śikhara* (now in ruins). The early Chalukya tank built in front of the temple is still in use.

Two other Chalukya sites that deserve to be noted are Naganathana Kolla and Huligemmana Kolla. The Naganatha temple at Naganatha Kolla is a structure built at the close of the 7th century AD. It is a Dravidian style temple noted for its outer wall decoration and the pillar sculptures in the porch along with the Ashthadikpalaka panels on the ceiling of the *sabhāmanṭapa*. The pillar sculptures in the porch are about 4 ft. in height. They are the earliest such pillar sculptures of the Chalukya period. They soon became an inspiration for such pillar sculptures found in the porches of temples like the Lad Khan, Huchchappayyagudi, Huchchappayamatha and the smaller temples in the Jyotirlinga group of temples at Aihole and the temples of Virupaksha and

Mallikarjuna at Pattadakal. In the early sixties of the 20th century, a large panel of Lajja Gauri was lying beside the temple. It is now shifted to the museum at Badami. This sculpture is by far the biggest and the most boldly carved sculpture of Lajja Gauri to be carved by the Chalukya artist.

Fig. 6.27. A memorial temple at Huligemmana Kolla.

The Huligemmana Kolla near Bhadranayakana Jalihal is another lesser known Chalukya site. Here, there are a large number of smaller monuments in the Kolla. According to one view, this was the place where the Chalukya king, Vikramaditya II, his queens and the ministers accompanying him were ambushed and killed. The monuments found here are supposed to be memorials erected to the king and others. The largest of the temples here is supposed to contain the relics of the slain king. (Fig. 6.26). On the wall of this temple is an inscription mentioning the relic's casket. The other smaller temples with only a sanctum and porch are said to be the memorials of the king's queens and other officers (Fig. 6.27). The site contains a few early Chalukya sculptures including the Saptamatrikas. We also find a figure of Lajja Gauri carved on the rock.

7

Early Chalukya Sculptures

Sheelakant Pattar

At the very outset, I concede myself that I am not a practising sculptor and so I do not know where the shoes of those ancient artists pinched. That which follows may be treated as an appreciation of an art lover.

It is rather customary to label art styles after the dynasties that fostered them. In a way it is convenient, though it is not really a classical approach. Interestingly, the art history of Karnataka reveals the fact that every dynasty has contributed an art style of its own, though in different degrees.

Tremendous is the sculptures crop of Chalukyan period. It rained for the sculpture harvest, so to say. Confining myself to the scope of this paper, only a few typical specimens, as felt by me, are appraised. An attempt is made to point out the salient features inherent in them.

The Chalukyas of Badami, who succeeded the Kadambas, occupy a prominent position in the cultural history of Karnataka. The period of the Chalukyas, from the middle of the 6th century to the middle of the 8th, may be considered as the formative era. It would not be wrong to say that the greatest contribution of this dynasty lies in the field of sculpture and architecture. The sculptural study of pre-Chalukyan phase is very much hampered due to the scanty availability of images. However, sculptural art had already germinated and its roots were held firmly in this soil. The Buddhist icons from Sannati and adjoining Andhra region, and the Hindu sculptures from Banavasi area, may be cited as notable examples of pre-Chalukyan epoch.

It was during the period of the Chalukyas that art and architecture enjoyed a sudden spurt. Thousands of images, big and small, belonging to different religious faiths, were chiselled to beautify excavated caves and structural temples, as well. The Chalukyan sculptors have rendered yeoman service in standardizing iconographical features of religious sculptures. Credit should go to the rulers and donors who patronized these constructions abundantly. Hence, the period is rightly regarded as the golden epoch in the art history of Karnataka.

The russet-coloured rocky hills not only acted as impregnable forts at Badami and Aihole but also beckoned the architects and sculptors to make use of these cliffs as the medium of their art expression. It is worth pointing here that the Chalukyas were the first southern power to build huge temples in massive scale in an imperishable material, i.e. stone.

These sedimentary hills near Aihole, Badami, Mahakuta and Pattadakal provided ample room for artists to scoop out rock-cut temples and to erect structural ones. The sculptors beautified them with a variety of images bringing dignity to this quardruple complex. These are more famous sites. Lesser known Chalukyan sites include Siddanakolla, Sulebhavi, Bhadranayakana Jalihal, Bachinagudda, Kelur, Nagral, Hunagund, Sandur, Itagi and Banavasi. The most important site in Andhra Pradesh region is Alampur, where there is a cluster of temples like Papanasanam, Satyavolu, Kudaveli, Mahanandi, Panyam Tondrapadu and Kadamara Kalava. Badami remained as the nucleus of art activites of all these places.

Among these, Pattadakal enjoys the status of being a World Heritage Site, where one can notice excellent sculptural representation and architectural perfection as well.

Some scholars hold the opinion that sculptural art of the Chalukyas is an offshoot of the Gupta style while others think that it has its origin in the art style promoted by Ikshvaku kings. But obviously, the Chalukyan art is indigenous and has its root in its own soil. However, there is a considerable amount of influence of the Gupta tradition and that of the Andhra art. How can art exist in a vacuum? An artist, being very receptive to the environment, gets influenced by the best he sees. This results into what may be called cultural diffusion and the Chalukyan art is a product of this phenomenon. It is largely indigenous and remains native to its soil, though it has amalgamated elements from other art traditions.

By and large, as we all know that Indian art, in its essence, is spiritual and the Chalukyan art is no exception to it. The massive and prime images are generally those of gods, the majority of them being Hindu. The rulers have exhibited Catholic taste by promoting Jaina and Buddhist art traditions also.

The religious sculptures speak of the heavenly world as revealed by the ancient scripts. Like the Jataka stories in Buddhist tradition, *Bhagavata* episodes and those of *Ramayana* and *Mahabharata* provided themes for the sculptors. The narrative panels in Cave II and Cave III are the earliest representations in the Deccan. The epic themes being religious became more popular and pillars of the Virupaksha at Pattakadal are profusely carved with such scenes.

But, an artist cannot neglect the affairs of the world he lives in. Every aspect of contemporary social life finds expression in his art. Activities of the mundane world are delineated in the motifs providing ample opportunity to infer the life of the period. The beauty and variety of fauna and flora have been the theme of decorative reliefs. Fables from the *Panchatantra* are depicted on stone for the first time. Thus, the Chalukyan sculptors are the pioneers in carving scenes from the Hindu ancient texts.

The sculptors adopted two kinds of techniques in carving the images. Craftsmanship involed in executing sculptures in cave temples is different. Here, the image at hand is immovable. An artist cannot tilt or angle it in a position that is required. On the other hand, he himself has to turn or twist to chip away unwanted part of stone, whereas, while preparing an icon to be installed in a structural temple, the sculptor works on a free block of stone that can be lifted, shifted, tilted and placed in any comfortable position to enable carving. He is deprived of these opportunities in decorating rock-cut temples.

As the cave excavation begins from the top edge, artists undertake the ceiling work first. Carving a figure on the ceiling is the toughest job. I cannot imagine how the ancient sculptors managed to do it, because one has to face the ceiling while chiselling. This means that eyes were at risk of being hit by tiny flakes of even small particles of stone. What kind of protection did they have for their eyes, is still a mystery.

Artistry of Michelangelo in the use of brushes and paints against earth's gravity on the ceiling of Sistine Chapel in Italy in the 16th century is much spoken of by art critics all over the world, but no appreciation of Chalukya sculptors is recorded with regard to their chiselling work on the ceiling of the rock-cut temples, almost one thousand years before Michelangelo.

Another constraint that the sculptor in cave excavation is confronted with is that he has no opportunity of replacing any part. In some of the figures of cave temples, we notice tips of noses or lips or earlobes are chipped off. We do no know whether it was due to a flaw on the part of an artist while at work or an act of vandalism. As they were very much used to carve on the walls and pillars of caves, they at times followed the same procedure in structural temples too. They installed huge pillares in their respective places and then carved low bas-reliefs on them. In the same way in some places and then carved on blocks of stones after there were set in the wall. Half-finished sculptures of Sangamesvara temple at Pattadakal are good testimonies.

The second method was to carve an image in a separate place and after the completion, it was placed in the wall or niche. The beautiful figures in the niches of Durga temple are of this type. Probably, final touch was given after housing them in niches.

However, it appears that artists found it more difficult to set the well-finished or half-done sculpture in the wall without being damaged. So they preferred to carve narrative reliefs on the pillars and blocks of walls, after they were positioned in their respective places.

The special features that make Chalukya sculptures unique are as under. In the first instance, the images are varied. The art creation in terms of quality and quantity is extraordinary. They are simple in composition, yet artistic and imposing. The balance and poise maintained therein is eye-catching. The main figure in the composition is artistically finished and presented relatively in a bigger size. The minor figures like those of attendants are depicted in smaller sizes and comparatively coarse in treatment and texture. Thus, the concept of centrality is observed in Chalukyan sculptures. The very principle of protagonist was adopted earlier in Ajanta art, where Buddha is shown in titanic form while his disciples are carved in miniature size.

In sculpting icons of gods, the artists have attempted to express grace of divinity on the faces. One can notice sublime bliss on Nataraja's countenance in Cave I and serene look on the face of Bahubali in Cave IV at Badami.

For the sake of convenience, we may classify early Chalukya sculptures as under:

1. Colossal sculptures
2. Man-sized sculptures
3. Medium-sized sculptures
4. Small sculptures
5. Miniature sculptures

Let us examine these categories briefly one by one.

COLOSSAL SCULPTURES

One can see colossal images in the rock-cut temples at Badami. They are the representations of gods belonging to different faiths. These massive sculptures are suggestive of divine might. They differ from each other in style, composition and presentation.

For example, in the composite figure of Harihara in Cave I, the spouses of Hari and Hara are depicted in their respective places. The space berween Parvati and Siva is occupied by his vehicle Nandi, while that of Lakshmi and Vishnu by Garuda. The fact that Parvati and Lakshmi sculptures are very much similar in ornamenataion, drapery and anatomical bends of feminine limbs, speaks of artistic excellence. This happens to be the earliest example of Harihara in the site. One more massive image of Harihara was carved, after about a couple of decades in Cave III. The composition is without concerts and vehicles. Thus, novel iconographical presentation can be noticed. This form came into vogue in due course of time.

The same kind of phenomenon can be noticed in the iconographical development of Ardhnarishwara sculpture. The execution of this figure in Cave I is superb. The way in which the sculptor has blended masculine and feminine anatomical features is of high order. Steadfastness of Bhringi has been the theme of this narrative panel. Bhringi stands in the form of skeleton to the proper right of this composite figure of Ardhanarishwara and on the other side is a lady attendant with charming beauty. While one implies death, the other suggests life. Both of them are not blissful. The God shown between them is full of eternal bliss. This appears to be the message of the artist. The subsequent icons of Ardhanarishwara lack these details, and only the composite form is retained.

The Chalukya rulers patronized all religious faiths. They firmly believed that all physical forms are manifestation of the same god. The main objective of such composite figures is to bring unity and harmony among different sects.

The earliest images of Bahubali (Gommata) and Parshvanath in south India are found in the caves of Aihole and Badami. These figures are more narrative in representation. Bahubali is shown with his sisters Brahmi and Sundari serving him. And Parshwanath is attended by Dharanendra and Padmavati. Subsequently, icons gained simpler forms leaving off the details of narration, thus contributing to the development of Jaina iconography.

The huge figures in cave temples are generally shown with suave faces, thick lips, blunt nose, plump cheeks and broad chest as in the case of Mahavishnu in cave III. There is a wide range of variety in stance and position while carving Varaha or Trivikrama sculptures.

It is quite interesting to note a different countenance in the colossal images of Cave I and II at Badami. In the Shaiva cave, the eyes of Harihara or *dwarapalaka* are fish-like and are linear in expression, whereas the eyes in the images of Cave II exhibit a different style. Here the eyes are half-closed, as it were, suggesting contemplation. This makes us think that the artists involved in execution of these icons belonged to a different stock. As these figures are after the style of northern Deccan, it appears that possibly the sculptors of the Malava region were brought in here as opined by Dr. S.V. Padigar. This view is supported by the names of sculptors on a boulder close to Cave II. The label inscriptions are in Siddhamatrika script, while the other names are engraved in Kannada script.

MAN-SIZED SCULPUTERS

This category is also mainly comprised of divine figures. The important art creations at Ravalpahdi cave at Aihole reveal many life-sized sculptures. Of them, the icon of Nataraja (Mahanata) catches our attention most. He is shown dancing with ten arms in the company of Saptamatrikas. These appear to be the earliest examples of this kind and yet they are the most exuberant and perfectly executed sculptures. These man-sized images are very much stylized and are decorated with rich ornaments and attire. Crowns worn by the mothers being exceptionally elongated, form a type of their own. A unique ornament called Vaikakshaka is worn by the Matrikas. This unique ornament appears to be very much in vogue in the sixth century in Ajanta region too. Interestingly, this ornament is not found in the eight century Chalukyan sculptures.

Of the life-sized figures, the dancing Siva in Cave I at Badami is widely applauded. This icon is popularly known as Nataraja. He is referred to as Mahanata also. The high bas-relief has many artistic merits. The sculptor has masterly executed eighteen arms in limited space. Nataraja is identified as having assumed 'Chatura' Natya posture.

It is a known fact that the concept of Nataraja sculpture has a spiritual message. His cosmic dance symbolizes five divine acts, namely creation, preservation, destruction, giving rest or illusion and grace or salvation. These, when considered separately, are the activities of Brahma, Vishnu, Rudra, Maheshwara and Sadasiva, respectively. His dance is regarded as the wheel of the universe and his arms as spokes.

Akshamala, i.e. garland of beads stands as a symbol of 36 principles. The drum that produces primordial sound is a token of creation. Act of preservation is indicated by the lifted two hands holding a serpent, the symbol of mite. His grace is expressed through a trident that emancipates devotees from worldly bondage.

Apart from its spiritual significance, the sculpture of Nataraja is credited with artistic value. The eminent dancer Sundari Santanam has identified as many as nine classical movements called 'Karnas'. It is quite interesting to note that mathematical permutation of arms reveals 81 postures of body.

Man-sized sculptures can be noticed in significant numbers in the structural temples of Pattadakal, which represent the last phase of Chalukyan sculptural art. Of them, the outstanding example is the one we find in the blind porch of Galaganath temple. It is a lively depiction of Andhakasura Samhara with eight arms wielding weapons. Lord Siva is shown in the act of slaying the demon, Andhhakasura. A trident is thrust into the body of the demon. Siva's poise is suggestive of his immense strength. The entire panel is a superb work of craftsmanship.

The *dwarapalas* in the Virupaksha temple at Pattadakal are figured in life size, and are full of energy. They look ferocious with their eyes opened and eyebrows raised, as if enquiring the entering devotees. Of all the *dwarapalas,* the one in the southern porch of the temple is outstanding. It looks as if it is an independent sculpture. But actually it is a part of the very pillar. This masterpiece is executed by Baladeva, the son of Duggi Acharya. He has also carved an image of *dwarapala* installed in the porch of Papanatha. It appears that Baladeva had specialized in carving *dwarapala* figures.

As soon as one enters the ASI museum at Aihole, the beholder is captivated by the marvellous work of art depicting the figure of Kushmandini (Ambika) in life size. The elegance and beauty of the image is beyond verbal expression. This piece is a product of high technical skill and artistic calibre.

MEDIUM-SIZED SCULPTURES

It is but natural that the number of sculptures inversely varies with the size. Less is the size, more are the sculptures. Accordingly, numerous medium-sized images, say, about 1 m in height, can be seen in the Chalukya temples. With this size, it would be more handy to chisel the details of composition.

This group of medium-sized sculptures is comprised of bas-reliefs of gods, amorous couples, *dwarapalas* (doorkeepers), Salabhanjikas and so on. The list of the divine sculptures of this kind would be too long. Siva and Vishnu images at Malegitti Sivalaya, Govardhana Giridhari of Upper Sivalaya in Badami, Ardhanarishwara, Varaha and Lakulisha figures at Mahakuta, Durga, Vishnu, Siva-Nandi sculptures of Durga temple are excellent pieces of artistry, to mention a few. All of these are housed in niches.

The sculpture of Ardhanarishwara icon in a niche of Sangameshwar temple at Mahakuta is yet another example of artistic excellence. The composite face of the deity looks graceful with knotted hairdo bearing the crescent moon and skull. Half of the third eye is delicately chiselled on Siva's side. Parvati's hand is shown as if playing with her curly hair. Below her breast, folds in the skin speak of the sculptor's creative mind. Round icon of Mahishasuramardini installed in a subshrine of Virupaksha temple at Pattadakal is another superb work of art.

The ceiling bas-reliefs of trinity of gods at Huchchappayyamath and Konti temple (Aihole), Nataraja images of Huchchppayya temple (Aihole) and Papanatha temple (Pattadakal), Kartikeya of Huchchinmalli temple (Aihole) and Surya of Virupaksha temple (Pattadakal) form a class of their own.

Ravana lifting Kailasa and Gajendramoksha have been the themes of outstanding narrative sculptures of pillars of Virupaksha temple (Pattadakal). The scenes are dramatically expressed.

Amorous couples are solidified in the brackets of Cave III at Badami. These are the enhancing pieces of art. Still more sensational are the couples on pillars of Mallikarjuna and Virupaksha temples at Pattadakal. Those at Nagral and Aihole too are noteworthy.

These figures express amorous feelings in a dignified way. Nowhere do we find perverted sex displayed in such *mithuna* representations.

Interestingly, in a couple of *mithuna* sculptures at Aihole, a lady is shown with the face of a donkey. This reminds us of an old Sanskrit verse: *Praptesu Shodashe Varshe, Gardabhi Api Apsara Bhavet.* When a girl attains the age of 16 she, though as ugly as donkey, looks like a nymph.

The Salabhanjikas form yet another important group. In these figures the artists have tried to render feminine beauty in all its charm. The sculptor is very much aware of curvaceous female anatomy. The Salabhanjikas are shown with firm breasts, slender waist, broad hips and shapely legs. Natural beauty of these ladies gains an upper hand over the decorative ornaments as against Hoyasala art. The Salabhanjikas in Cave III at Badami are the earliest examples of this kind in the south. The tradition of Salabhanjika sculpture is continued in the subsequent periods.

SMALL SCULPTURES

Naturally, small sculptures are in a big number. Needless to say that these beautified architectural members like *adhishthana*, pillars, beams and ceilings.

Dwarf figures, the narrative panels depicting stories, *dikapals*, *nidhi devatas*, *nadi devatas*, *yalis* and *yakshas* have found their places here.

Frieze of dwarfs on the *adhishthana* of rock-cut temples and structural temples has been a characteristic feature of Chalukya architecture. The theme of these figures is mainly reflection of the contemporary social life. Commoners are shown dancing, fighting, playing musical instruments, performing acrobatics or playing with snakes. In some of the dwarf figures, we notice complicated portrayal of human anatomy projecting their limbs in unusual directions and postures. The life of common man has been the main theme of these dwarf figures.

The beams in Cave II and III at Badami consist of small sculptures depicting stories from *Bhagavata* and *Harivamsha Purana*. These are the earliest representations of puranic episodes possibly inspired by the Buddhist art tradition of Jataka stories. Such narrative panels have found their place in the *adhishthanas* of structural temples like Upper Sivalaya and Durga temple.

Ramayana reliefs and *Mahabharata* illustration on the walls of Papanatha and pillars of Virupaksha make a room for special study.

Decorative sculptures such as griffins or *yalis*, *vidyadharas* and celestial nymphs are carved on beams, brackets and ceilings. The drapery and ornamentation of the flying celestial figures as well as their bends in limbs and stretch of arms greatly resemble the ones in Ajanta art.

Animals like elephants, lions, horse, etc. have been the theme of small sculptures. They reflect the characteristic behaviour of particular animals. On the *adhishathana* of Papanatha porch, we find interesting scenes showing two elephants attacking a lion and two lions attacking an elephant. A pillar in Mallikarjuna temple (Pattadakal) bears a figure of a tamed elephant carrying a long log of wood. The angularity of log speaks of balance maintained by the elephant. The sculpture is realistic in depiction.

MINIATURE SCULPTURES

Miniature sculptures are basically decorative and not thematic in purpose. They are generally found on the pillars and door jambs. As a matter of fact, sandstone is not a good medium for carving delicate or tiny figures. Yes, the craftsmanship of Chalukya sculptors is commendable. A good number of Lilliputian figures have been shaped. Mithuna figures in miniature size have found a place in door jambs as seen in the Durga temple. Needless to say that these carvings are based on strict measurements.

Such decorative sculptures exhibiting fauna and flora are generally done in low bas-reliefs. Hundreds of small circles, semi-circles, triangles, and rectangles are made to emerge on the surface of the stone. The ceiling of Ravalphadi is rich with such decorations.

The above classification is only for the sake of convenience. There can't be a line of demarcation. They are intermingled and intertwined. The artists conceived them comprehensively. As a result, they could achieve complexity and integrity, blended with beauty.

The study of architects and sculptors of the region would make a room for special survey. Names of about half a dozen architects have appeared in contemporary inscriptions, outstanding of them being Saravasiddhi Achari, who is described as Vastu Pitamaha, the Father of Architecture. Gunda Anivaritachari enjoyed the title Tribhuvanachari, Revadi Ovajja, who conceived Papanath temple, was a disciple of Sarvasiddhi Achari, Aryaminchi Upadhyaya of Badami was the architect of Malegitti Sivalaya, and Narasobba of Aihole is adored as 'Shastra Maheshwara'.

Label inscriptions found in and around the monuments have revealed the names of more than hundered sculptors. Beyond doubt, unknown artists are more in number.

About 60 names occur on boulders near cave temples. They have been identified as the names of carvers. The only sculptures autographed by the artist are that of Garuda image on the eave of Cave III at Badami. The artist happens to be Nelavarke.

A good number of sculptures in structural temples bear the names of sculptors. Of them, Baladeva, Devaputra, Chengamma, Pullappa of Pattadakal and Ganasobba, Krichunga of Aihole deserve high appreciation.

The earliest available Kannada literary work of 9th century titled *Kavirajamarga* describes the folk of Karnataka as having an innate trait of composing poetry without reading poems. In the same way, the Chalukyan sculptors exhibited a sense of experimentation in carving icons, not strictly adhering to norms of iconography as laid by ancient texts.

8

Mahakuta: Lesser Known Early Chalukya Art Centre

Meena M. Mohite

INTRODUCTION

In the history of south Indian architecture and iconography, the early Chalukyas of Badami stand out by their pioneering efforts in supporting vigorous religious building activity. They founded a large number of rock-cut and structural temples, scattered over Karnataka and Andhra Pradesh.

In Karnataka, the monuments of the early Chalukyans are found at Aihole, Badami, Pattadakal and Mahakuta. Apart from these centres, we find their monuments at Siddhanakolla, Sulebhavi, Jalihal, Benakanavari, Huligemmanakolla, Subbalahunasi, Kelur, Naganathanakolla and Hungund in Bijapur district, Kumarasvami Hill near Sandur in the Bellary district, Ittagi in Raichur district and Banavasi in the Uttara Kannada district. In Andhra, they are concentrated in what was then the Chalukya *Vishaya* comprising the present Kurnul and Mahboonagar districts. The prominent temple sites are Alampur, Papanasanam, Satyavolu, Kudaveli Sangama, (now the temple is shifted to Alampur in view of the building of a dam across river Krishna), Mahanandi, Panyam, and Kadamara Kalava.

The present paper aims at giving a brief account of the temples built in Mahakuta. An architectural survey of temples at Mahakuta has been studied in detail since no detailed studies are available with a view to evaluating the significance of these temples in the broader context of early Chalukya art and architecture. It may be noted that most of the studies done so far relate to the temples at Aihole, Badami, Pattadakal and Alampur.

MAHAKUTA

Mahakuta is located in Badami taluk, of Bagalkot district, in the state of Karnataka. It is located at 75°-44′ E. Longitude and 15°-57′ N. Latitude. It can be reached from Badami, via Kendur, which is about 8 km in distance. It can also be reached from Badami, through Banashankari via Shivayoga Mandira. This distance is about 18 km. Mahakuta is a beautiful place laid out with lush green orchards, plantations and fields. The Mahakuta *kshestra* is situated amidst horse-shoe shaped hills filled with lush greenery and naturally grown medicinal plants. The best of parrots, peacocks, foxes, and rabbits are of daily acquaintance here.

While going from Shivayoga Mandira to Mahakuta, on the way we come across a historical site assigned to the period of the early Chalukyas. It is known as Hale Mahakuta. It is also known as Chikka Mahakuta. Here we find three temples, one tank, known as *koti tirtha* set amidst horse-shoe-shaped hillocks. The oldest temple is the apsidal Siva temple. To its south, we have two temples with different architectural elements, joined together. The apsidal temple, which is of early Chalukya period, is in a dilapidated condition with its *śikhara* lying in debris near by.

About 1 km towards Hosa Mahakuta on the right side, among coconut plantations, we find two temples—Adikesvara and Bhairaveshvara.

As was the tradition, at Mahakuta too, temples are located around water sources. The early Chalukya temples are always located near a water source like a well or a tank or a pond or a river. Mahakuta has two important *tirthas*. Chikka-Mahakuta also has a *tirtha* nearby called as *Koti tirtha*. In the Mahakuta complex, all the 18 temples of *Rekha Nagara, Dravida,* and *Kadamba*

Nagara styles are situated around a holy tank called Vishnu *puskarani.*

Temples at Mahakuta Complex:

1. Mahakutesvara
2. Mallikarjuna
3. Nataraja
4. Bhadravalinga
5. Somesvara
6. Veerabhadresvara
7. Kalakalesvara
8. Agastesvara
9. Lakulisvara
10. Kotilinga
11. Bhimesvara
12. Ramesvara
13. Pinakapani
14. Vyagrahapadesvara
15. Chandrakesvara
16. Kannesvara
17. Sangamesvara
18. Virupaksesvara

Temples outside the complex within Mahakuta:

1. Bananti gudi
2. Hire Mahakutesvara
3. Adikesvara
4. Bhairavesvara
5. Apsidal Siva temple

Temple Plans

We find more than half a dozen types of plans. These are:

1. Temples with a *garbhagṛiha* and porch.
2. Temples with *garbhagṛiha, sukanāsa, prdakshiṇāpatha, sabhāmanṭapa,* porch and *Nandi Manṭapa.*
3. Temples with *garbhagṛiha, sabhāmanṭapa, pradakshiṇāpatha,* porch and *Nandi Manṭapa.*
4. Temples with *garbhagṛiha,* and porch with railings.
5. Temples with *garbhagṛiha,* and porch without railings.

6. Temples without niches.
7. Temples with only a sanctum.
8. Apsidal temple. It includes an apsidal *garbhagṛiha,* apsidal *pradakshiṇāpatha, sabhāmanṭapa* and porch.
9. Secular structure.

The type of plan and its size as well as its decoration depended upon the finances of the patron.

Main Features of Mahakuta Temples

Adhishṭhāna

A characteristic feature of the early Chalukya temples is the *adhishṭhāna.* The upper part of the latter generally bears a *kapōta* moulding. Almost all the *kapōta* mouldings at Mahakuta are characterized by *kuḍu* motif, human figures, peacock, etc. as surface decoration. In the Sangamesvara temple, we also have the *Ślesha* motif representing the bull and elephant, accommodated, on the *kapōta* moulding.

The *kumuda* is another feature very characteristic of early Chalukya *adhishṭhānas.* At Mahakuta, three types of *kumudas* are seen. These are *vṛitta kumuda, tripaṭṭa kumuda* and multifluted *kumuda.* The *vṛitta kumuda* is seen in the Makutesvara temple, the *tripaṭṭa kumuda* is seen in the temples of Kalakalesvara, Kannesvara, Pinakapani, Sangamesvara, etc., and the multifluted *kumuda* is seen in the Somesvara temple. However, it is observed that *tripaṭṭa kumuda* was the most preferred mode as was the case in many early Chalukya temples elsewhere. We have *jagati* in the form of *padma* moulding, for example, in the temples of Mahakutesvara and Mallikarjuna.

Another feature of the early Chalukya *adhishṭhāna* at Mahakuta is the presence of a broad *gaḷa,* either plain or carved. The Kalakalesvara, Agastvesvara and Hire Mahakutesvara have plain *gaḷas.* Hire Mahakutesvara has a broad *gaḷa.* The *gaḷa*s in the Mahakutesvara and Mallikarjuna at Mahakuta, like those in the Huchchappayyagudi at Aihole and Melagitti Sivalaya at Badami are carved with miniature reliefs. Scenes from the *Rāmāyaṇa, Mahābhārata,* sporting elephants, and some other miniatures are found carved in the *gaḷa* of the above-mentioned

Adhiṣṭhāna: Mallikarjuna Temple

Adhiṣṭhāna: Mahakutesvara Temple

temples. At Mahakutesvara, the story of *Ravānanugrahamūrti* found in the basement is well known to art historians. These miniatures portray the following events: 1) Ravana lifting Kailasa, 2) Ravana engaged in penance, 3) Ravana offering his own head as *bali*, and 4) Shiva blessing Ravana. In other words, the *gaḷa* was utilized to depict narrative sculptures.

Decoration of the Wall

We find three types of walls:

1. Walls which are plain
2. Walls with projections and recesses
3. Walls with projections and recesses with *kōshṭhas*

Description of Sculptures

The temples in the Mahakuta complex and the Rashtrakuta temples nearby exhibit remarkable sculptures. These sculptures are varied and ever interesting, and occupy a prominent position in the annals of Chalukya art. We know that Saivism rose to importance in the second phase of Chalukya art and most of the images at Mahakuta are connected to Saiva mythology. Some of these represent Narasimha, Harihara, Ardhanarisvara and Lakulisa. There are a large number of Lukulisa sculptures indicating the large following that Lakulisa had at Mahakuta.

Aspects of non-religious art also can be seen in the temples at Mahakuta. The numerous *mithunas* in various erotic postures described in Sanskrit literature assumed immense importance and became a popular motif. The Chalukyas made a liberal use of this motif on shafts, brackets of pillars, doorjambs, etc. For the first time, *maithuna* was depicted in the temples at Mahakuta and it was later continued in Pattadakal temples. It became bolder in theme in the later Chalukyan temples, such as the one at Bagali. This was a period of transition from early to medieval times in the depiction of the erotic motifs.

Thus, in both artistic and iconographic forms, the Chalukyas treated Puranic themes with unusual grandeur and vigour. It was the golden epoch of neo-Brahmanical art, when stone was transformed into the wisdom of the Puranas and the Agamas.

SCULPTURAL ART

We find sculptures carved on walls, *adhishṭhāna,* pillars, railings, ceilings, beams, and on doorframes. The sculptural art in Mahakuta temples can be studied as under:

a. Secular sculptures: Erotic
b. Sacred sculptures: Classical deities/Cult deities
c. Narrative panels
d. Loose sculptures

Description of the Main Temples

Mahakutesvara Temple

This temple at Mahakuta is the only early Chalukya temple, where there has been no break in worship since its construction. From the available Mangalesa's pillar inscription, which clearly mentions the name of the God, and speaks of endowments to the

God, it is clear that this site is in continuous worship from a few years prior to AD 602 till present times. It has unbroken 1500 years of history.

The temple faces east. The main entrance into the complex is exactly in front of the Mahakutesvara temple. In between the entrance door and the entrance of the main temple, we have an open *Nandi Manṭapa.*

This temple consists of a *garbhagṛiha, pradakshiṇāpatha, sukanāsi, sabhāmanṭapa* and *mukhamanaṭapa* in addition to a *Nandi Manṭapa*.

The Adhishṭhāna

The *adhishṭhāna* is considerably high. It comprises of *upāna, vṛitta kumuda, kapōta* and *paṭṭa,* which is horizontally divided into two sections. The lower section recedes while the upper section projects. This *paṭṭa* is carved with scrolls, floral designs, snakes and such other decorative motifs. Above the *paṭṭa* is a *gaḷa,* which is 16" high. The *gaḷa* is carved with narrative sculptures, *mithunas* and *apsaras.* Then comes the projecting *paṭṭa* carved with petals.

Window No. 1

Walls: The walls are decorated with corner pilasters and projecting *kōshṭhas* with double pilasters. We find four *jālandhras* on the southern side and four more *jālandhras* on the northern side. They are fixed into the *sabhāmanṭapa* and the *pradakshiṇāpatha*.

Each *jālandhra* is different from the other. These windows have a pilaster frame supporting an eave with a variety of shrines and *udgama* patterns. Starting from the north-east corner, we have the window no. 1: 3′ x 2½′ with *swastika* motif in centre and four squares up and down with crossed grilles. The eave has shrines in simple design.

Window no. 2 opens up in the second part of the *sabhāmanṭapa,* and is more decorative than the first one. The *swastika* motif in the first window is replaced by the crossed grilles all over and the grilles are decorated with diamond, bean and flower motifs. The pilasters, the eave and miniature shrines are similar to window no. 1.

Window No. 2 (north wall figure)

When we observe window no. 3, it is more evolved in terms of decoration. It is framed with small-sized pilasters, supporting an eave with cupola and *śāla śikhara,* miniature shrines with *kuḍus* with a face within. The entire entablature is supported by a *yaksa,* who is beautifully carved. The support of the *yaksa* is beautifully depicted. The *yaksa* carved below the eave is positioned as if to convey that he is supporting the entire superstructure represented by the *śāla* and the *kuḍus* above the cave.

Window No. 3 (north wall)

The window no. 4 on the northern side is again very decorative. However, the

Window No. 4

upper *vimāna* decoration is replaced by *Udgama* motif with a *kuḍu* and a split *kuḍu*.

Similar windows are placed on the southern side. However, the design on the entablature depicts minature shrines, one more beautiful than the other, and at the same time the miniature *vimāna* shrines become more and more complicated.

This entire wall on all sides is topped by a curved eave with *hamsamāla* underneath, running all round the temple. A parapet runs above the eave, which is about 2 ft high. The *hāra* consists of *śālas* and *kuḍus*. There are some damaged and heavily painted images on the roof including Siva, Parvati and Brahma. These seem to be later additions. In short, the entire eave is crowned by a *hāra* made of *karṇakūṭas* and *madhyaśālas*, flanked in between by two pilasters and *kuḍu vimāna* motif.

DESCRIPTION OF THE WINDOWS OF MAHAKUTESVARA ON THE SOUTHERN WALL

The First Window on the Southern Wall

This window is framed by small pilasters, supporting a small eave, which in turn exhibits three layered *nasi*-motifs. The window has no decoration within.

The Second Window from the South

The pilasters and eave along with window design are same as that of the earlier window. However, changes are seen in the miniature *vimāna* shrines, depicted below.

Third Window on the South Wall

This window is differently decorated. The window is decorated with crossed grills, and the entablature of half-*kuḍu*-cut and *kuḍu* motif.

The Fourth Window on the South Side

This window portrays an entablature of *vimāna* designs, *Dravida śikhara* of cupola type with *nasi* in centre, the lower segment is same as third window, except the grills are placed by square openings.

Window No. 5

Window No. 6

DESCRIPTION OF THE SCULPTURES IN THE NICHES

Starting from the right side of the *manṭapa* wall, in the first *kōshṭha,* we have a sculpture of a Jatamandala Siva. He is depicted beautifully in *tribhanga* pose, with a long *triśūla* in the right arm and *sarpa* in the left. He is wearing *sarpakuṇḍala, patrakuṇḍala, yajñōpavīta* and *kaṭisūtra.* In the left side *kōshṭha,* we have an image locally called as Jatabhara Siva. He is shown with the third eye. He wears *kaṇṭi, kaṭisūrta, uttarīya, kēyūra* and *yajñōpavita.* As we proceed from the right side of

Window no. 7

the *manṭapa,* we find a *kōshṭha,* located on the south side of the *manṭapa* wall. It has a depiction of Bhikshatana Siva. He is in *tribhanga* pose, holding a *sarpa* in the left hand and *kapāla* in the right hand. He is wearing *hāra, pushpayajñ ̄opavīta, makarakuṇḍala,* and *patrakuṇḍala.* He wears *jaṭāmukuṭa,* with half moon in it. The sculpture is very attractive and proportionate. In the *garbhagṛiha kōshṭha,* we have another sculpture of Siva with third eye. He holds a *triśūla* in the right hand and the left hand is broken. He has *jaṭāmukuṭa, sarpakuṇḍala, patrakuṇḍala, kaṇṭi, kaṭisūtra, udarabandha,* with a snake tied as *kaṭisūtra* and other decorations. He is in *dvibhanga.*

At the back wall of the sanctum, in the western *kōshṭha,* we have a sculpture locally called Karanda Mukuta Siva. He is holding *triśūla* in the right hand, and *sarpa* in the left. He is in *samabhanga* with *nāgavōles.* He is depicted with calm and serene face. As we proceed to the northern side of the temple, in the *garbhagṛiha* niche, we find a beautiful sculpture of Ardhanarisvara in *tribhanga* pose.

The last *kōshṭha* on the *manṭapa* wall houses another sculpture of Siva with snake in his left hand and *paraśu* in the right hand in *dvibhanga* pose. The pilasters which house these sculptures are highly decorated.

Over the *garbhagṛiha* we have the *śikhara.* At the lowest level (for the new levels are later additions), we have the base of the *śikhara,* about 2 ft tall, with square sunken space all around. On this base we have a Dravidian *śikhara,* of *dvitala,* with *hāra,* carried on upper *tala* also. The *hāra* is decorated with *karṇakūṭa* and *śāla*. At the corner of the octagonal *grīva* are found *alpavimāna*, or four *karṇakūṭas* at the four corners and the central *kūṭas* depict *kīrtimukhas*. Then we have a huge octagonal *stūpi* surmounted by *kalaśa*.

Window No. 8

The *garbhagṛiha* is square. On plan it measures 3.35 m x 3.40 m. It is a *sāndhara* temple. The *sabhāmanṭapa* has a central nave and two side aisles, with slopy roof. The sanctum has a *linga* of rather very low proportions and practically no *piṇḍi*. This *piṇḍi* is classified as *Svayambhu linga*. It means that this *linga* is *jāgruta*, as it has come up on its own. The *garbhagṛiha* ceiling is flat and plain. Within, the sanctum is supported by huge, plain pillars, with two armed brackets, on all four sides, supporting the beams.

In the middle of the first two pillars, we have the sanctum doorway. This doorway has three *śākhas*. The first *śākha* is simple and plain. The second *śākha* is bigger than the first one and depicts erotic reliefs. However, these are painted in silver colour. The third *śākha* depicts a pilaster supporting an architrave, carved with *karṇakūṭa* and *śāla śikhara* motifs in a series of nine shrines. Above the series of *śāla sikharas*, we have square dentils. The *lalāṭabimba* depicts three figures; two of them are in *añjali*, worshipping the *linga* which is carved in the centre.

At the base of the door jambs, we have two figures in *añjali* pose on both the sides of the first *śākha*. Further, we also have sculptures on the bottom of the door jambs. On the left side of

Entablature and pilasters in Mahakutesvara temple

the door, we have small sculptures of about 12" tall of a lady under a parasol and a man with a *gaṇa* in between; on the other side, we have sculptures of a man, a *gaṇa* and a woman. Since these are darkened with soot, it is not possible to identify them.

The *sukanāsi* divides the temple into *sabhāmanṭapa* on the anterior side, and *garbhagṛiha* within. The *sabhāmanṭapa* is supported by huge *rucaka* pillars. In the ceiling of this *manṭapa,* we find a lotus with three concentric circles.

Outside the porch, pillars, four in number, are huge and plain, with an inscription on them. There is a lotus ceiling in the porch. The doorway of this porch is enclosed with golden coloured metal rafters.

Facing the temple in the east, there is an open *Nandi Manṭapa* with four pillars, and a large seated Nandi within. The *Nandi Manṭapa* is raised on a simple base and has a curved eave all around the raised flat roof. The lower parts of the pillars of the *manṭapa* are carved with erotic scenes in three quarters medallions.

The Mahakutesvara was a very important temple. There are more than six inscriptions related to this temple. The foremost and the most discussed is the Mahakuta pillar inscription of Mangalesa dated AD 602. This inscription reveals many issues related to religion and endowments. In fact, in the inscription itself, it is mentioned as *dharma-jayasthambha,* or Pillar of Victory of Religion.

First of all, it enlightens us that this place of worship was in existence even before Pulakesi-I's time, as in line 13... it says, "was assigned by our father and elder brother"... its antiquity can be easily pushed back to the first half of the 6th century AD.

Śikhara (Mahakutesvara)

It mentions the name of the god as 'Makutesvaranatha', ... in line 13. His mother came from Batpura family and was religiously motivated.

From other inscriptions, we can gather that endowments continued to flow in and through 7th century, 8th century and 10th century it continued to be a place of worship. After the re-establishment of the Chalukya power at Badami in AD 655, the earliest inscription available is that of Vinapoti's. She is described as the *prāṇavallabhe* of Vijayaditya.

The next inscription is that of Bappavarasa dated AD 934, carved on a pillar in the *mukhamanṭapa.* It mentions that Bappavarasa, who held the high post of *sāmanta,* came all the way from *kaṭaka* and donated lands from Nandikesvara to the god. This shows the importance of the place even during the 10th century.

The next most important inscription is the inscription of "Puttimaninaga". This inscription is also located on a pillar in the *mukhamanṭapa*. It was first noticed by Fleet, but it was not translated. However, he commented that he thought it was

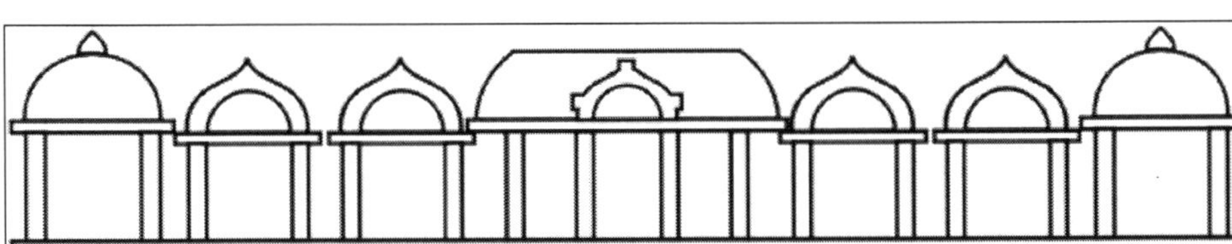

Hara

palaeographically similar to the one at Pattadakal in the Virupaksha temple.

However, in 1981 it was observed that there was a duplicate of this record, not in the Virupaksha but in the Galaganatha temple. Unfortunately, only the temple was related to Vinayaditya's period, and as no other instance of a duplicate inscription is found, Dr. Carol concluded that the date of the Mahakutesvara is AD 675–750 based on the paleography of this Kannada record.

However, recent studies of this inscription throw different light altogether. (See, Kannada University Epigraphical Series: IX, Bagalkot District, page no. 341, Mahakuta, inscription no. 400, and page no. 223, Pattadakal inscription No. 104, on a pillar in the Sangamesvara temple.)

A translation of the inscription, on the pillar in the porch of the Mahakutesvara temple, states that it belongs to the reign of Jagattunga, a Rashtrakuta king, and further states that the king's feudatory, a certain Uttamagalla, participated and killed 1966 men with his *kaditale* (a shield). It is a 9th century AD record.

The inscription, on a pillar in the Sangamesvara temple at Pattadakal, refers itself to the reign of Jagattunga, probably a Rashtrakuta king, and states that the king's feudatory, a certain Utamagalla, participated and killed 1966 men with his *kaditale* (a shield). It is a ninth century AD record.

The above inscription is of the 9th century AD and it no longer supports Dr. Carol's dating of the Mahakutesvara temple to Vinayaditya's period. Instead, we can say that Vinapoti's inscription is the earliest inscription in the temple. She was a favourite concubine of Vijayaditya. She must have got special interest to donate to the temple which was probably rebuilt during her patron's period. Therefore we can assign the date of this temple to Vijayaditya's period. Secondly if we go by Dr. Carol's logic, then Sangamesvara is Vijesvara, built during Vijayaditya's period. Therefore, the dating of Mahakutesvara will fall in Vijayaditya's reign. (AD 669–AD 733)

THE MALIKARJUNA TEMPLE

This temple is situated in the north-west corner of the Mahakutesvara complex. It is facing east and dedicated to Siva. It is built of sandstone with a Dravida Śikhara. It is a *sāndhara* temple.

The plan of the temple consists of a *garbhagṛiha,* with *pradakshiṇāpatha,* a *sabhāmanṭapa,* a *mukhamanṭapa* and a Nandi *Manṭapa.*

The plinth of the temple consists of a *upāna, kumbhaka, tripaṭṭakumuda, kapōtatilaka,* which shows *gandharvas* and *kinnaras.* Birds like *mayūras* and *cakravākas* with intricately and exquisitely done florid tails appear between the *nāsis.* The *pāda* begins with *pratikanṭa* and auxiliary mouldings, from which *simhavyāla* and *gajavyāla* are carved with *kinnaras, vyāla* riders on the upper mouldings and *vidyadharas* at the *karṇas.* The plinth is completed by mouldings of the *ardha padma* petals.

WALLS

The walls possess projections and recesses, with huge *kōshṭhas* and *jālandhras* flanked by pilasters. The pilasters are decorated on the base. We have three pilasters followed by a *jālandhra,* then a *kōshṭha* flanked by four pilasters, two on each side with an image in it. Thus, we have three *jālandhras* on each side, and two sculptures, with one more sculptures on the back of the sanctum wall. Below the eave, one can observe *hamsamāla* going all around. This eave is topped by a *hāra* with *kūṭas* and *śālas.*

Before we go into the details of the *kōshṭha* images, we must note that the plinth makes provision for narrative sculptures as in Mahakutesvara temple. These narratives are carved in *gaḷa* of less height than at Mahakutesvara temple. These portray interesting deities like *asṭha-dikpālas;* lion-headed, human-bodied, Narasimha with four arms; Ugra Narasimha; standing Vishnu; seated Siva; seated Nagaraja; *mithunas* and Visnu riding Garuda surrounded by warriors. At the back of the sanctum on the *gaḷa,* we have beautiful depiction of *gaṇas.* On the west side, we can identify Vishnu, Brahma and Siva in their courts. A few panels in between

The *Śikhara* of Mallikarjuna temple

contain erotic reliefs. The last panel on the west wall has a beautiful depiction of Trivikrama.

In the *kōshṭhas* at Mahakutesvara temple, we have exclusive Saiva images, but this temple contains Vaishnava images. These were all carved into the masonry *in situ*. In fact, on the hills, behind Mahakutesvara complex, we located an entire piece of wall of a temple lying there. From this, we could gather that the entire *kōshṭha* with four pilasters and recesses and projections formed one unit. The image was carved with the unit lying on the ground, and after completion it was fixed in its place.

In the north side *kōshṭa* of the *sabhāmanṭapa,* we have a sculpture of Vishnu, who is four-armed with *cakra, śaṇkha, bīja*, and hand on hip. The north niche image has a four-armed Ardhanarisvara; the male right side has an axe in the upper hand; and the lower hand is resting on a long-haired *gaṇa* carved below, while in the female half, the upper hand touches her earrings; her falling sash is held by the lower hand. The relief in the central west niche shows Siva holding an axe and a snake in his upper hands and a rosary below with the other hand on his hip. He is accompanied by two female dwarfs. The south *sabhāmanṭapa* niche has Siva, whose attributes are snake (upper left), on hip (lower left), axe (upper right), and trident (?) lower right. The next niche on the south side of the *sabhāmanṭapa* has a sculpture locally called Sthanaka Brahma. Here the god is standing in *samabhanga*, with four arms holding a rosary and a *ḍamaru* in the upper arms.

The lower left hand is holding a *sarpa* and the right hand is holding a pot.

In all, we have six windows, two opening into the exterior *manṭapa*s and the third one opening into the *garbhagṛiha*, on one side, the same is repeated on the southern side. These windows like the Mahakutesvara *jālandhras* are beautifully decorated with small entablatures sporting series of *vimāna* designs. The difference is that these windows are not flanked by pilasters, but the entablature is supported by stronger frames of the windows themselves. The window design show grills crossed over, square openings, and the last window on the western side depicts a *matsya chakra* (fish-wheel motif). The upper sides of the windows are decorated with finely carved intricate miniature shrines each different from the other.

As said earlier, *hamsamāla* appears below the *kapōta*, running all around, which is topped by a *hāra* with *kūṭas* and *śālas*. The *hāra* is systematically sequenced by *karṇakūṭas*, with three *kuḍu* pilasters with blind windows, followed again by *karṇakūṭa*, three *kuḍu* pilasters, and *madhya śālas*.

We have a fine Dravidian *śikhara* on the *garbhagṛiha*. Though it appears like the *śikhara* of the Mahakutesvara, it has some vital differences. The octagonal *śikhara* is of the *tritala* variety with eight *kuḍu* shrines.

The base of the *śikahara* has an *upāna*, which is broad, and a small *jagati*. On this we have pilasters flanking blind windows, topped by three *kūṭas*, and the same is again repeated with three units of *karṇakūṭa*, *śāla* and *karṇakūṭa*.

On the last rung, the huge octagonal *śikhara* is held by *kuḍu* shrines on eight sides with sculptures within. These sculptures are indistinct.

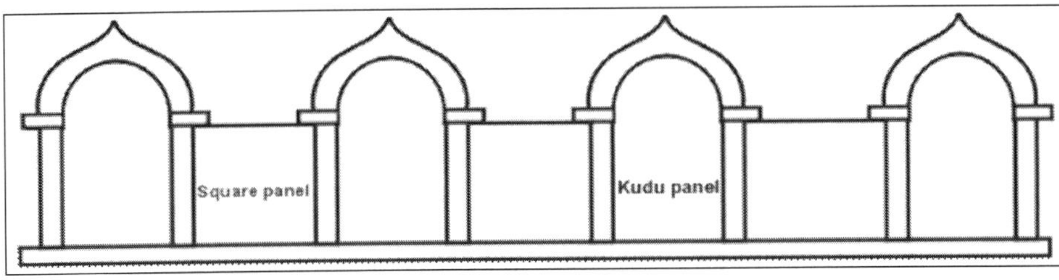

Sabhāmanṭapa

The *garbhagṛiha* is square on plan housing a huge *linga* and is supported by pillars with four armed brackets. The pillars are plain *rucaka* pillars.

The sanctum doorway is divided into four *śākha*s, with the third *śākha* in pilaster form. The second *śākha* is decorated with diamond and bean pattern; the first *śākha* is decorated with scroll motifs. In the *lalāṭabiṁba,* we have a Garuda with snakes, holding the tail ends, and these snakes are sliding down the side of the door and emerging as Nagas with seven hoods on both sides and in *añjali* pose.

The pilasters at the end of *śākha*s are supporting a horizontal eave, with geese, supporting the *pratsara* above. The *pratsara* is decorated by shrine motifs of *śāla* and *kūṭa* in one line at the bottom and above it has figures of *gaṇas* in *śāla* and *kūṭas.*

The arrangement of the pillars is such that the hall is divided into a central nave and two side aisles. Unlike Mahakutesvara beams, these are located east-west, rather than in north-south orientation. The distance between the beams on the pillars and the ceiling is highly extended, giving a space all round, almost 4′ 11″. Thus, the total height of the ceiling from floor is 14′ 11″. The pillars themselves are 10′ in height.

The entire *sabhāmanṭapa* is supported by geese motif all around. Above it, there are plain blind windows, followed by panels, with pilasters and *kuḍu* motifs (as shown below).

Description of the *sabhāmanṭapa* upper side panels: Starting from the left side, from the *garbhagṛiha,* we have ten big square panels, alternated by pilaster *kuḍu* panel.

1. Square panel	:	A woman and two men, *gaṇa*-like in appearance with the lady lying on the ground, with her legs up, and the man is shown in an excited mood.
2. *Kuḍu* panel	:	A woman in *samabhanga.*
3. Panel	:	Two men and a woman in centre.
4. *Kuḍu* panel	:	A man in *samabhanga.*
5. Panel	:	A musical scene where two men are playing different musical instruments,

			while the man in the centre is enjoying the music.
6.	*Kuḍu panel*	:	A man.
7.	Panel	:	*Gaṇas* with the one in the centre has the face of Nandi.
8.	*Kuḍu* panel	:	A woman.
9.	Panel	:	Men in group, one of them holding a sword while another holds a *ḍamaru.*
10.	*Kuḍu* panel	:	A woman.
11.	Panel	:	Ugra-Narasimha?
12.	*Kuḍu* panel	:	A man.
13.	Panel	:	A *kinnarī* in the company of a *gaṇa.*
14.	*Kuḍu* panel	:	A man.
15.	Panel	:	Two men, of whom one is doing penance.
16.	Panel	:	Three *gaṇa*s making merry.
17.	Panel	:	Indistinct, due to darkness, but *gaṇa*-like figure is seen.

The study of the above panels reveals that the themes are associated with Siva. The *gaṇa*s, *ḍamaru*, and *Nandigaṇa*, indicate that this entire panel was reserved for *gaṇa*s, the mythical supporters of Siva, who were always near him.

This panel is followed by a panel showing five elephants on the march in addition to *kuḍus.*

On the right hand side, the theme in the panels differs. Here, we have Mahisamardini panel, erotic panels, and common social day-to-day life events. The panel of *kuḍu* alternated by elephants is found on the right side too.

From the side panels, we now go to the ceiling. For the first time in this area of study, we come across beautifully decorated ceiling panels in the temple. We have three beautifully decorated ceiling panels. The first one is a Siva and Parvati, the second one is of Brahma, and the third one is of *gandharvas.* The first ceiling panel depicting Siva and Parvati is located near the sanctum door, thus indicating the Saiva character of the temple.

Here, Siva and Parvati are seated upon an energetic and leaping Nandi. The figure of Nandi is depicted as robust, and shown diagonally in the square. This central Siva-Parvati panel is surrounded by three square borders. The first square border has floral designs. The second square border is bigger having beautiful lotus. The last one is a big square depicting *gaṇa*s in a row, in different postures. In the Nandi-square, we notice two *gaṇa*s have been accommodated below Nandi and one *gaṇa* above Siva and Parvati in the centre.

The next panel is situated in the centre of the *sabhāmanṭapa*. This square panel is divided into an equal nine smaller squares. The central square has Brahma seated on a lotus. He is four-armed holding a rosary in the right and the left arm is in the *abhaya-mudra*. The lower left hand is broken, and the lower right hand rests on his thigh. *Rishis* with pointed beards flank him. The four squares in the four corners are decorated with lotus flowers. The alternate squares on all sides are carved with images of Indra, Varuna, Agni and Yama. The divisions of the big square into small squares are done by intricately carved thin lotus ribbons.

The next panel is located nearer to the main entrance. This is again divided into nine squares. In the centre we have a very big and beautiful lotus with small lotuses at the corners, within the squares. The alternate squares are filled with beautiful flying *gandharvas* in pairs, holding a sword and shield and embracing a female companion.

The Mukhamantapa

This *manṭapa* is supported by huge pillars, marked by full medallion on the shaft with *taranga pōtikas*. The first two pillars of the porch have two large sculptures on both sides. On the pillar nearer to the entrance steps, we have a short man, in high relief, partially bald, and leaning on a thick stick with one hand on its top and the other grasping it near the top. He is dressed in short *dhōti* and sandals. His long curly hair falls on to his shoulders. The figure on the other pillar holds a stick in the same way; wears a long *dhōti* wrapped with a heavy sash, and a cloth cap over his head. Both have a dagger at the waist and a sword hilt appearing over the shoulders, and each sports a moustache. Their identity is an intriguing question. The identification of these figures as Agastya and Tolkappiyar is unconvincing.

On the east, facing the central entrance, we have the *Nandi Manṭapa* with a counchant Nandi. It is the most well-decorated *Nandi-manṭapa* of the place, and also the best preserved.

The pillars of the *manṭapa* are square with *taranga* brackets. The shaft is decorated with half medallions in the upper and lower parts. However, we can observe in the upper part of the shaft a pillow-like band. The half medallions are beautifully decorated with floral designs.

CONCLUSION

The Chalukyas have played a significant role in the history of south Indian art and architecture. Their political history falls into two clear-cut phases, but the cultural history exhibits three centres of movement.

The first phase witnesses the rise of the Chalukyas under Pulakesi I and the rapid expansion of the kingdom under his successors—Kirtivarma-I, Mangalesa and Pulakesi II. Under Pulakesi II, extensive conquests were undertaken. By AD 635, they held command over a large area. Along with political power, much attention was provided to building activities, and the study of these monuments in the first phase exhibits the adoption of cave architecture for propagating Vedic culture and traditions. A few Buddhist traditions were also followed.

The second phase starts with the restoration of the early Chalukya power by Vikramaditya-I, son of Pulakesi II in AD 655. This period witnessed the zenith of Chalukya political power and cultural achievements under Vikramaditya-I, Vinayaditya, Vijayaditya and Vikramaditya-II. This phase is marked by the rapid development of structural architecture. Cave architecture was given up. Construction of temples meant greater scope for architects and sculptors to exhibit their techniques, skill, vision and creativity.

However, at this juncture, I will make it clear why I say three cultural phases or cultural movements. In between the period of interregnum, the political power was shifted to Chalukya Vishaya. This area came under the effective control in Pulakesi II's rule. In the Tummeyamuru grant, which cannot be later than AD 637, a reference has been made to Lord Sangamesvara. As sequence to this was the founding of a branch known as the Vengi Chalukyas in AD 624. Thus, the control of Andhradesa seems to have been effective since Pulakesi II's time. Adityavarma-brother of Vikramaditya, governed the principality of Chalukya Vishaya.

The study of the architectural activity at Alampur demonstrates that the local school of Alampur is not a derivative of the traditions of the temples of Pulkesi's time at Aihole and Badami. The Arka Brahma placed in the first stage of development has an inscription of Vikramaditya. The Vira-Brahma and the Bala-Brahma exhibit close architectural elements with Arka Brahma and thus Vikramaditya's support cannot be ruled out. However, the Kumara-Brahma lacks particular mannerisms from Aihole and suggests the peculiarity of the Alampur guild of artists. Thus, in the first stage, the Chalukyas continued to support cultural activities at Aihole, Badami. The Svarga-Brahma temple is securely dated to Vinayaditya's time. Further, on the basis of the architectural and sculptural aspects, the Siva temple at Panyam and Mahanandisvara temple at Mahanandi are assigned to Vinayaditya's period. One more inscription of Vijayaditya at Alampur is important as it records the construction of an enclosure wall to the temples at Alampur by the pontiff Isanacanya in AD 713. Thus, Alampur was the second cultural centre.

The third cultural centres are Mahakuta and Pattadakal. These two places emerged as great Saiva centres, with all the temples dedicated to Siva. The latina shrines at Mahakuta show closer similarity to Kumara-Brahma temple at Alampur. The Kumara-Brahma reveals a refinement as well as advanced features over early Nagara temples at Aihole. This makes it clear that local guilds had their own designs and inspirations. The *latina* shrines at Mahakuta are to be dated in the restoration period. In the rich cultural enterprise, the royalty or nobility and the priestly order contributed or play a significant role. To this aspect, we possess definitive epigraphical evidence. The Amudalpadu plates of Vikramaditya refer to the *Siva mandala diksha*. The preacher Sundarshanacharya is mentioned as the recipient of the gifts. This important event must have led to the inauguration of temple-building activities at Alampur, for this place had by then attained political importance. In the second half of the restoration period, Mahakuta and Pattadakal emerged as great centres of Saiva religion. At Pattadakal, a new adherence to religion was made by the sectarian pillar of Kirtivarma-II. The inscription mentions it as a *triśūla-stambha,* which became a landmark and attracted visitors from far and near.

In Mahakuta, building activity started with the replacement of the brick temple of Mahakutesvara with a stone temple in the closing years of the 7th century AD. This was followed by the construction of temples with *Rekha Nagara śikharas.*

This building activity at Mahakuta started with the renovation of the main temple of Mahakutesvara sometime between AD 700 and AD 720. In fact, there is a possibility that the entire earlier temple in brick was replaced by a new temple with *garbhagṛiha, pradakshiṇāpatha, sabhāmanṭapa* and *mukhamanṭapa.* On stylistic and architectural grounds, this temple can be placed at the end of the 7th and the beginning of the 8th century. As far as antiquity is considered, it is the earliest temple to be referred in the inscriptions of the Chalukyas. The Mahakuta pillar inscription reveals that it was a great place of religious import and antiquity.

We find about six inscriptions in this temple alone. Except the Mahakuta pillar inscription, the rest of the five inscriptions do not mention the name of the deity, while giving donations. We can therefore surmise that this was the only well-known temple of the place. The rest of the temples, including the Mallikarjuna, were built in the later part of the restoration period. To be precise, some of them were constructed during the period of Vikramaditya-II and his successor. The study of the sculptures reveals that we have thirteen sculptures of Siva. The syncretic forms of Siva, namely Ardhanarisvara and Harihara are special. The Ravana's episode with Siva is highlighted in miniature reliefs in the Mahakutesvara temple. The chiselling of a rare iconographic form of *Urdhvaretas* about six in number, indicates the imaginative bent and religious zeal of the Chalukyan artist. Aspects of non-religious art can also be seen here in the form of *mithuna* and *maithuna* sculptures. Decorative arts like flower motifs, geometrical designs, *pattas*, and medallions were used liberally. Due to their variety, style and ornamentation, the Chalukyan sculptures occupy a prominent position in the annals of the Deccan art.

9

Marketing the Golden Ring of North Karnataka

Vandana Palankar

NORTH KARNATAKA

North Karnataka is relatively an arid plateau, at a height varying between 300 and 700 metres in the state of Karnataka in South India. Rivers Krishna and its tributaries, the Bhima, Ghataprapha, Malaprabha and Tungabhadra flow through this region. It mostly lies within the Deccan thorn scrub forests, which extends to the north into eastern Maharashtra.

North Karnataka includes the present districts of Belgaum, Dharwad, Uttara Kannada, Bijapur, Bagalkot, Bellary, Koppala, Gadag, Raichur, Yadagiri, Gulbarga and Bidar. The Major cities and towns in this region are Hubli-Dharwad, Belgaum, Bellary, Raichur, Gulbarga, Bidar, Bagalkot, Gadag and Karwar.

North Karnataka's contribution to literature, art and architecture and music is too well known. It is also known for its social reformers, freedom fighters and educational institutions.

North Karnataka is known for its temples belonging to various creeds and religions. These monuments belong to Jaina, Hindu, Buddhist and Muslim religions. Aihole is often referred to as the cradle of Indian architecture because of the variety and styles of temples found there. These temples, mosques and mausoleums belong to Kadamba, early Chalukya, Rashtrakuta, Kalyana Chalukya, Sevuna, Vijayanagara, Bahamani, Adil Shahi and Bidar Shahi dynasties. The well known art-sites of north Karntaka are Mahakuta, Aihole, Badami, Pattadakal, Kukkanur, Sudi, Gadag, Dambal, Kuruvatti, Haveri, Hangal, Bankapura, Chaudadanapura and Huli to name a few. Hampi and Pattadakal are listed as World Heritage sites.

HISTORY OF NORTH KARNATAKA

Pre-historic Period of North Karnataka

North Karnataka's history and culture date back to the pre-historic period. At Sangankal archaeologists have unearthed earliest village settlement of South India, which belongs to the Neolithic period. Stone implements of the Palaeolithic and Neolithic periods are found in many places in North Karnataka. The early inhabitants of North Karnataka were using iron implements, which can be dated to about 1200 BC. These iron implements have been discovered at Hallur during excavations.

There are rock shelters in the districts of Raichur, Bellary, Koppal and other districts in north Karnataka where pre-historic paintings are found. Some of these rock shelters are found at Kurgod and Hampi in Bellary District, Hire Benkal in Koppala District and Badami in Bagalkot District. These paintings reveal human figures, wild animals, etc. These are painted in red. In many places in north Karnataka, Megalithic remains have been discovered. Hire Benkal is famous for these megalithic remains. On the hill at Aihole, a large number of dolmens, now in ruinous condition, can be seen.

Historic Period

North Karnataka was ruled by many dynasties. The presence of Asokan edicts reveal that a major part of Karnataka was ruled by The Maurys. Chandragupta Maurya is said to have spent his last days at Sravana Belgola. The royal families of the Satavahanas, early Kadambas, Badami Chalukyas, Rashtrakutas, Kalyana Chalukyas, Hoysalas, Sevunas, Vijayanagara, Bahmanis, Adil Shahis, Barid Shahis, Kutub Shahis, and others have left behind a treasure house of material related to paining, art, architecture, and development in different fields of culture.

MAJOR TOURIST ATTRACTIONS OF NORTH KARNATAKA

The following is a select list of historically important places in north Karnataka: Aihole, Badami, Mahakuta, Pattadakal, Banashankari, Banavasi, Sandur, Bellary, Bidar, Gulbarga, Firuzabad, Bijapur, Dharwad, Lakkundi, Gadag, Haveri, Hangal, Annigeri, Dambal, Hampi, Raichur, Kuruvatti, Sannati, Unkal, Sudi, Ron, Konnur and Bankapur.

BUDDHIST MONUMENTS

The following are the well-known Buddhist monuments: Tara Bhagavati Temple at Ballegavi in Shimogga District; Koliwada and Dambal in Gadag District; Kanaganahalli and Sannati in Gulbarga District, where remains of ruined stupas and plaques of Satavahana period have been discovered recently in addition to sculptures; the half-structural and half-rock cut storeyed Buddhist Chaitya at Aihole belonging to the Badami Chalukya Period (Fig. 9.1); at Badami in between Caves II and III, there is a rock shelter and on the rock are found a few sculptures which have been identified as Buddhist sculptures. One of these has been identified as of Bodhisattva Padmapani. To the present day belong the Tibetan settlements at Mundagod in Uttara Kannada District, where stupas and painted prayer halls are built. Recently, at Gulbarga two new stupas—one big and the other small—have been built.

Fig. 9.1. Two-storey Buddhist chaitya.

Shakti Sthalas

North Karnataka is known for quite a number of *Shakthi Sthallas*. Pilgrims visit the temples built in these *Shakti Sthalas*. These include the temples of Chandralamba in Sannnati, the temple of Bhagavati in Ghattaraki, the temple of Mayavva in Chinchli, the temple of Yellammma at Saundatti, the temple of Banashankari at Banashankari near Badami, the temple of Pampadevi (Bhuvanesvari) at Hampi, the temple of Marikamba at Sirsi, and the temple of Mukambika at Kollur.

BADAMI (VATAPI)

Badami, formerly known as Vatapi, is a taluk in the Bagalkot district of Karnataka, India. It was the capital of the Badami Chalukyas from AD 535 to 757. It is famous for rock-cut and other structural temples. It is located in a strategic place in a ravine at the foot of a rugged, red sandstone outcrop that surrounds the Agastya tank.

The name Vatapi has its origin in the Vatapi legend of *Ramayana* relating to Sage Agastya. There were two demon siblings, Vatapi and Ilvala. They used to kill all mendicants by tricking them in a peculiar way. Ilvala, the elder, would turn Vatapi into a ram and would offer its meat to the guest. As soon as the person ate the meat, Ilvala would call out the name of Vatapi. Vatapi had a boon that whenever Ilvala calls him he would return from wherever he was. Vatapi would come out of the belly of the person who had eaten him, thus killing him. This trick worked until Sage Agastya countered them by digesting Vatapi before Ilvala could call for him, thus ending the life of Vatapi. Two of the hills in Badami according to the legends represent these demons.

History

1. Badami was the capital of the Early Chalukyas between the 6th and 8th centuries AD. They succeeded the Kadambas.
2. The early Chalukya rule was founded by Pulakesi I in about AD 535. His sons Kirthivarman I (AD 567-598) and his brother Mangalesha (AD 598-610) enlarged the kingdom by conquests.

Fig. 9.2. Caves of Badami.

They were also responsible for excavating the caves at Badami.

3. The greatest among the early Chalukya rulers was Pulakesi II (AD 610-642). The Aihole insrcription mentions in detail his conquests including his defeating Harshavardhana the ruler of Kanauj. He also fought with Mahendravarman I, the Pallava ruler of Kanchi.
4. The rock-cut Badami Cave temples were carved during the 6th century. The four cave temples represent the secular nature of the rulers and their tolerance to people belonging to other religions including Jainism and Buddhism.
5. Among the cave temples at Badami, Cave I (Fig. 9.3) is dedicated to Siva; Caves II and III are dedicated to Vishnu (Figs. 9.4 and 9.5) and Cave IV to a Jaina Tirthankara. Deep caverns with carved images of the various incarnations of Hindu gods are strewn across the area, under boulders and in red sandstone. From an architectural and archaeological

Fig. 9.3. 18-Armed Nataraja outside Cave 1, Badami.

perspective, they provide evidence of the early styles and stages of development of Karnataka architecture and the process of standardization of iconographical features of various deities.

Culture

The main language of the early Chalukya period was Kannada though the copperplate charters of the royal family are in Sanskrit. The local population wears traditional Indian cotton wear.

Geography

Badami is located at 15°55′ N 75°41′ E / 15.92°N 75.68°E / 15.92°; 75.68°. It has an average elevation of 586 m (1922 ft). It is located at the mouth of a ravine between two rocky hills and surrounds Agastya *tirtha*, a water reservoir on the three other sides. The total area of the town is 10.3 sq. km.

It is located 30 km from Bagalkot, 128 km from Bijapur, 132 km from Hubli, 30 km from Aihole, another ancient town, and about 500 km from Bengaluru, the state capital.

Climate

- Spring - January to March
- Summer - March to June
- Monsoons - July to October
- Winter - November to January

The temperature ranges from a minimum of 23 degrees to a maximum of 45 degrees during summer and from 15 degrees

Fig. 9.4. Trivikrama in Cave 3.

Fig. 9.5. Vishnu image in Cave 3.

to 29 degrees in winter. The average rainfall of the area is 50 centimetres. The best time to visit is from November to March.

Badami is also known as a habitat for monkeys. The cool climate has made it a safe haven for the monkeys. Tourists often flock to Badami for an opportunity to see monkeys interact in a natural environment.

Economy

The main economy is based on tourism and agriculture.

Transport

The nearest airports are Hubli and Belgaum about 120 km and 150 km, respectively. Badami is on the Hubli-Sholapur rail route, and the

Fig. 9.6. Sidlaphadi.

Fig. 9.7. Temple at Naganathakolla.

rail station is 5 km from the town. It is also connected by road to Hubli and Bijapur. Badami is reachable from Bengaluru by a 12-hour bus ride, or by a direct train, or with a combination of an overnight train journey from Bangalore to Hospet followed by a short bus ride from Hospet to Badami. Another train journey could be from Bangalore to Hubli (8–9 hours) and then a bus ride to Badami (3 hours). Badami is around 120 km from Hubli. Local transport is by auto-rickshaws, tongas and city buses.

Fig. 9.8. Bhuthanatha temple at Badami.

AIHOLE

Aihole, which can be called a town of temples, is in Bagalkot District. It is a very popular tourist spot in north Karnataka. It lies to the east of Pattadakal, along the Malaprabha River, while Badami is to the west of both.

Aihole has the potential to be included as a UNESCO World heritage site.

HISTORY

Early inscriptions call this town Āryapura and Āyyavole. According to mythology, Aihole is the place where Parashurama washed his axe after killing the Kshatriyas. Aihole has historical and architectural significance. It is often referred to as the cradle of Indian Temple Architecture. The place is full of temples numbering more than 100 in addition to rock-cut temples. Aihole was the first capital of the early Chalukyas. Here, the early Chalukyas built more than 70 temples in different styles of architecture. Some even refer to Aihole as a laboratory of experiments in architecture. Pulakesi I moved the capital to Badami, which was then known as Vatapi, where he built a strong fort. The first phase of temple building in Aihole dates back to the 6th century AD, the second phase up to the 12th century AD. The temple building activity continued unabated even after the fall of the early Chalukyas.

Some well-known temples: A group of three temples called Kontigudi group of temples are built in *manṭapa* style. Another temple is the Lad Khan temple (of the late 7th or early 8th century AD), named after a mendicant that lived in this temple in the 19th century. Other temples of note are Huchchappayyagudi and the Huchchappayya *Matha* (Fig. 9.34).

Fig. 9.9. Durga temple at Aihole.

- Lad Khan temple (Fig. 9.11) consists of a shrine built within a large square pillared *manṭapa,* which is enclosed with walls and large stone grills. The sanctum has a Shiva linga. The hall in which the sanctum is built against the back wall has a total of 12 carved pillars, which are massive and square. The *sabhāmanṭapa* has pillars arranged in such a manner as to form two concentric squares. The temple looks like a village panchayat hall indicating that it was in the beginning used as secular structure. Later, a sactum was added.

- Huchappayyaudi has a *rekha nagara śikhara* over the sanctum (Fig. 9.32). The interior of the temple has beautiful carvings including a host of *gaṇas*. The temple was built by an architect named Narasobba. He was aided by Ganasobba, a sculptor.
- Huchimalligudi at Aihole, built at the beginning of the 7th century, is a typical early Chalukya temple showing a sactum, a *pradkshiṇāpatha*, a *sabhāmanṭapa* and a porch. There is a *rekha nagara śikhara* above the sanctum.
- The Galaganatha group of temples has nearly thirty temples on the bank of the Malaprabha river. The main shrine of the Galaganatha temple belongs to the nagara style with a *kadamba nagara sikhara*. It has images of Ganga and Yamuna on the door jambs.
- The Durga temple or temple in the fortress is the best known of the Aihole temples (Fig. 9.9). It is apsidal in plan, like most of the Buddhist caves in western India. It has a high basement. On plan it has an apsidal sanctum, completely closed apsidal *pradakshiṇāpatha*, a *sabhāmanṭapa*, a small porch in the front and all these sections of the temple are surrounded by half opened apsidal *pradakshiṇāpatha* leading to the entrance on the front. On the outer walls of the temple, there are niches filled with beautiful sculptures of Siva, Vishnu and Mahishamardini. The temple was built during the rule of Vikramaditya II. The temple was dedicated to Surya.
- Melgudi is a Jain basadi built on a hillock. It is the only dated monument built in AD 634. It is a storeyed *basadi*. The upper sanctum was an afterthought. From the roof, one can get a fine view of the temples built in the village. The temple, which

was possibly never completed, is an example for early Dravida architecture. The dated inscription found on the outer wall of the temple records the construction of the temple by Ravikeerthi, a poet in the court of emperor Pulakeshi II. Interestingly, the epigraph mentions Kalidasa and Bharavi, the well-known Sanskrit poets.

Fig. 9.10. Inside the Ravana Phadi cave.

- The Ravana Phadi cave is one of the five rock-cut caves in Aihole and is located south-east of Hucchimalligudi (Fig. 9.10). This temple dates back to the end of 7th and beginning of the 8th century, possessing sanctum, *antarala,* followed by a pillar-less *navaranga,* which is flanked by rectangular-shaped cells. There is a Shivalinga in the sanctum. This cave is noted for its sculptures. The ten-armed Nataraja is one of the finest sculptures of the early Chalukyas. The other sculptures found on the walls are those of Mahishamardini, Harihara, Gangadhara, Varaha and Dvarapalas. The Ravanaphadi has a *Nandi* platform and a monolithic *dharma stambha* behind the *Nandi* platform.
- The Gowdaragudi, which is square on plan with a sanctum built in the middle of the pillared hall, was probabaly built by the Ayyavole Guild since Durga Bhagavati was the patron deity of the Guild. An inscription in the temple mentions Durga Bhagavati, the patron deity of the Ayyavole Guild.
- The Suryanarayana temple has an image of Surya in the sanctum. The temple has a *rekha nagara śikhara.*

Fig. 9.11. Lad Khan temple.

The *mahanasika* has a damaged figure of Surya in it. The Surya image in the sanctum is of the Later Chalukya period. The temple built in the 8th century has a sanctum, a *sabhāmanṭapa* and a porch.

- There is a museum in the Durga temple complex maintained by the Archaeological Survey of India. Loose sculptures found in the temples and the village have been preserved here. One of the finest sculptures of the period found here is that of Ambika, which was originally in the Melgudi.

PATTADAKAL

It lies on the banks of the Malaprabha River in the Bagalkot district. It is 22 km from Badami and about 14 km from Aihole. It is well known for its historic temples.

World Heritage Site

The group of 8th century AD monuments in Pattadakal represent the zenith of early Chalukya art and architecture. Pattadakal with these temples was designated as World Heritage Site in 1987 by UNESCO (United Nations Educational, Scientific and Cultural Organisation). The site gets its significance because of the temples in both Nagara and Dravida styles of architecture, which is unique.

Tradition has it that the early Chalukya rulers were crowned in this place, hence the name Pattadakal. There are ten temples including a Jain *Basadi* surrounded by numerous small shrines and remains of plinths (Figs. 9.12 and 9.15).

The oldest temple at Pattadakal is Sangamesvara built by King Vijayaditya (AD 697-733). The other notable temples at Pattadakal are the Kadasiddhesvara, Jambulinga, Galaganatha, Virupaksha, Mallikarjuna, Galaganatha, Chandrasekhara and Papanatha. The Sangamesvara, Virupaksha and Mallikarjuna possess *Dravida śikhara* while the Galaganatha, Jambulinga and Kasivisvesvara

Fig. 9.12. A section of temple complex at Pattadakal.

Fig. 9.13. Carvings on a pillar of Virupaksha temple.

Fig. 9.14. Jain Narayana temple.

possess *rekha nagara śikhara*. The Kasivisvesvara temple was the last to be built.

The Sangamesvara, originally known as Vijayesvara after its builder king Vijayaditya, was the first of the early Chalukya temples to be built at Pattadakal, which was also known as Pattada Kisuvolal and Raktapura. The temple is noted for its *Dravida śikhara*, which is of the pure form, i.e. it does not possess a projection on the front. A notable feature in the temple is the separate provision made for installing the images of Ganesha and Mahishamardini in the form of niches outside the sanctum. The *manṭapa* in front of the temple is quite large and is supported by basically square pillars, which look massive. The outer walls of the temple possess large-sized sculptures, mostly Saiva in nature.

There are two temples at Pattadakal, which were built during the time of Chalukya king Vikramaditya II. His two queens, Lokamahadevi and Trailokyamahadevi, both uterine sisters, built the Virupaksha, originally called Lokesvara, and Mallikarjuna, originally known as Trailokyesvara, to commemorate the conquest of Kanchi, the Pallava capital on three occasions by Vikramaditya II. The Virupaksha was built under the supervision of the architects Gunda Anivaritachari and Sarvasiddhi Achari. Reputed sculptors like Chengamma, Baladeva, Pullappa, Aditya, and others worked on the sculptures found in the temple. Sculptures like those of

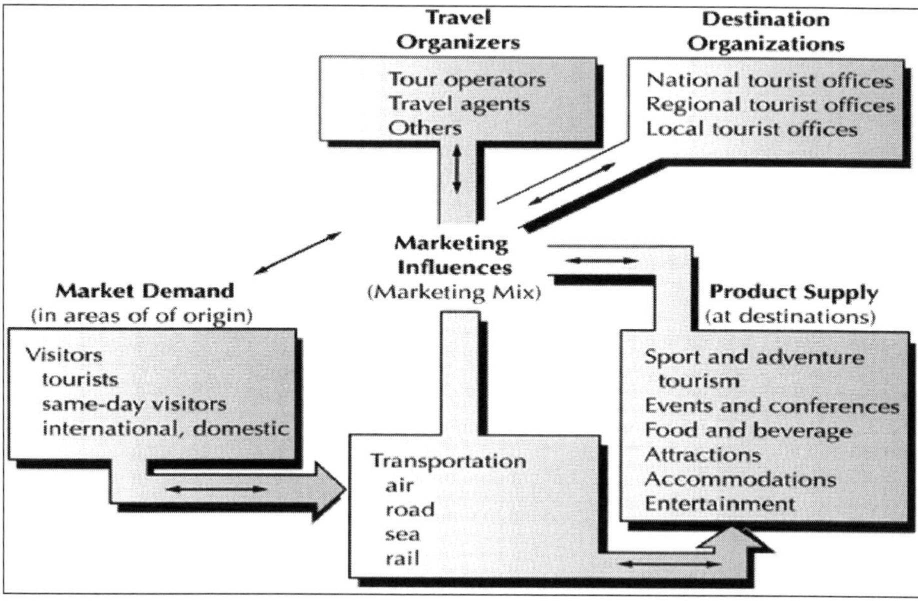

Transport infrastructure and physical access to destination

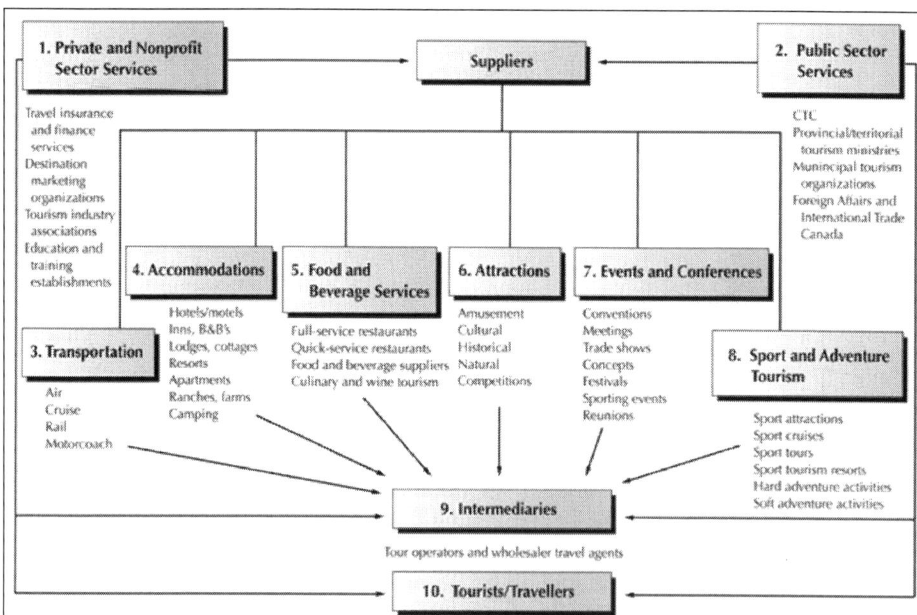

Key players

Limgodbhava Siva, Nataraja, Ravana trying to lift Mount Kailasa, and the Dvarapalas are some of the best early Chalukya sculptures ever to be prepared. The Virupaksha temple is supposed to have inspired the architects and sculptors who created the megalithic Kailasanatha temple at Ellora. The pillars inside the Virupaksha temple are noted for the narrative sculptures of the period. The pillars are embellished with small reliefs narrating the *Mahabharata*, *Ramayana*, *Gangavatarana* and other Puranic themes (Fig. 9.13). The Mallikarjuna temple is more or less a temple which duplicates whatever is found the Virupaksha temple in addition to royal couples carved on the inner side of the walls in the pillared hall, which are unique to this temple. Both the Virupaksha and the Mallikarjuna temples are of the Dravida order.

Fig. 9.15. Mallikarjuna and Kasivisvanatha temples built in 740 CE.

The Papanatha temple, built during the time of Kirtivarma II, was constructed under the supervision of the architect Revadi Ovajja, a disciple of Sarvasiddhi Achari. This temple with a *rekha nagara śikhara* is chiefly notable for the *Ramayana* panels carved on the outer walls of the temple. As in the Virupaksha temple, here too, the sculptors have inscribed the names of the characters depicted in the *Ramayana* panels.

The Jaina *basadi* (Fig. 9.14) at Pattadakal, locally called Jaina Narayana temple, was built during the time of the Rashtrakuta ruler Krishna II. Recently, the ASI has rebuilt the *basadi*. This *basadi* is a storeyed one with the upper sanctum built into the *Dravida śikhara* of the temple, which rises over the lower sanctum.

PRESENT SCENARIO

Key observations after the site survey:

1. Badami offers an incomparable experience of our past culture and antiquity. Situated in a picturesque countryside at the mouth of sandstone ravine, Badami symbolises a treasure-

house of architecture and temple sculpture. Just opposite to the caves is a small shop for light refreshments, which is not a standard/ decent one and affects the beauty and serenity of the place.

2. Sidlaphadi is a curious natural structure—a rock bridge of sorts with a hole in the centre (Fig. 9.6). The bridge has some gaping holes that are believed to be created by lightening. The name Sidlaphadi roughly translates to a cave formed by lightening. Here, ASI had discovered a few evidences about the bridge having sheltered prehistoric men. The ASI museum in Badami has a replica of the bridge and a few informational posters about way of life of the then inhabitants. It is an ideal trek spot and further from Sidlaphadi we can trek to Mahakuta. The only drawback is that there are no directions or markings to help the trekkers.
3. Aihole, the earlier capital of the Chalukya kings, is located at a further distance of 14 km from Pattadakal and the first experimentation of temple construction with stone blocks have been attempted here. It also houses a museum of ancient artefacts and sculptures. It is a typical setup for a remote village turned tourist spot. There is an enclosure within which exist early Chalukya temples restored and managed by the ASI. The Durga temple has a semi-circular apse and sanctum circled by a richly carved colonnaded passage way. Aihole has over 100 richly carved temples. It is a memorable visit that one would cherish for long though a bit tiring, having to climb the rocks and extensively cover by foot inside the vast expanse of temples.
4. On the outskirts of Badami, at a distance of 5 km, is situated the Banashankari temple of Chalukya period, with a big tank built opposite the temple named Harischandra Teertha. The presiding deity is Banashankari. The Banashankari fair runs for well over a month.
5. Pattadakal is situated at a further distance of 22 km from Badami, which was used as a second capital of the Chalukyas and was mainly intended for coronation of kings who ascended the throne.
6. The condition of the roads is very bad in most of the places and leads to a displeasure in the experience.

7. Not many trash bins can be found at many places.
8. Information brochures/folders printed by KSTDC contain facts that need to be rechecked on the authenticity of information.
9. There is no travel information or booking office at Badami and very limited bus connectivity to major places around.
10. Some of the sites around Badami are not considered at all (Fig. 9.7).

THE MARKETING PLAN

(1) Objective: To present Badami-Aihole-Pattadkal as an attractive tourist destination
(2) Factors affecting marketing effort

SWOT Analysis

Strengths

1. Badami and early Chalukya architecture
2. More than 45 species of medicinal plants in Badami-Mahakuta area are found
3. Pattadkal is one of the World Heritage sites
4. Aihole is well known for its temples
5. Banashankari and Kundalasangama are two other prominent piligrimage places nearing BAP ring
6. Hubli is the nearest place to connect
7. Natural landscapes and historical prominence is abundant

Weakness

1. Poor infrastructure
2. Road transport under-developed
3. Travel agencies do not promote these destinations mainly due to lack of proper infrastructure
4. Limited or no signage on important routes
5. No markings for trekkers near Sidlaphadi; very few know this
6. Maintenance of monuments

Opportunities

1. Resources and culture
2. Place of educational interest

3. Easy accessibility
4. A good adventure spot
5. Easily coverable within three days

Threats

1. Government's limited role in development
2. Lack of safety and security measures
3. Low awareness levels about the places, especially domestic tourists of other states
4. Limited Government bus services
5. Low marketing efforts by national and local tourism organizations
6. Lack of standard support services
7. Accommodation facilities are limited
8. Limited involvement of locals

(3) Market identification (segmentation): Schools/College/Tourism students, domestic and international tourists interested in historical, and adventure spots
(4) The marketing strategies (or mixes) for different markets you target—the best combination of the 4 Ps (product, price, place, promotion) for each segment (to be determined by NTO, RTO, tour operators, accommodation and transportation services)
(5) The marketing budget, implementation plan, method for evaluation and change to be followed by the respective organizations after step 4

Efforts have to be made by all the key players towards the achievement of the stated goal. As tourism is a complex industry, no single business/industry can alone contribute in its success. However, individual recommendations are cited in this research.

RECOMMENDATIONS

ITDC

- Has to provide support in the development of these regions at a national level
- Highlight the core benefits of the destination at all the prime fairs and road shows

KSTDC

- Take a keen interest in the development of these sites
- Introduce standard outlets in front of the Badami caves for refreshments
- Provide good support services, such as guides, route maps, etc.
- Build the infrastructure in terms of road transport and rail connections
- Highlight Hubli as a connection hub for flying public
- Introduce information desks at bus stands, airports and public areas across neighbouring cities and towns
- Provide with good directional markings for trekkers around Badami
- Aid the hoteliers in providing efficient services
- Local home stays can be encouraged
- Employ local people in providing vital informatory services, train them, so that it can help in employment
- It can also hold events and conferences in these places to attract visitors and create awareness
- Have a good number of outlets in important places to supply mementos
- Encourage handicraft business locally
- Provision of a good number of and well-maintained toilets/ washrooms
- Provision of potable water and trash bins everywhere
- Brochures/folders must be designed with relevant information and maps and has to be prepared by art historians
- Develop and promote some important sites which are almost forgotten like Huligemmana valley, which has memorials of Vikramaditya II and his wives
- In association with ASI promote medical tourism around Badami

ARCHAEOLOGICAL SURVEY OF INDIA

- Look into the monuments/sites, which can be promoted as interesting places around BAP circle
- Provision for sale of mementos at every site

- Provide with attractive package tours suitable for every segment
- Co-ordination with KSTDC and other services in the area
- Inclusion of tonga service as an attraction in the destinations
- Include attractive entertainment schemes to attract different segments of travellers
- Tie up with educational institutes and major firms to cater to their travel needs cost-efficiently
- Highlight rock climbing, trekking and cycling as adventure activities
- Open an office at Badami/Pattadkal to facilitate travellers.

HOTELIERS

- Mobile canteens at several locations

OTHERS

- Rent a cycle service
- Handicraft outlets
- Mobile emergency services
- Beauty, spa and other recreational services

MONUMENTS/SITES NEEDING SPECIAL ATTENTION

HULIGEMMANA KOLLA (VALLEY) (Figs. 9.16 to 9.29)

Fig. 9.16. View of Huligemmana Kolla.

Fig. 9.17. Memorial temple for Vikramaditya II, Huligemmana Kolla.

Fig. 9.18. Inscription on the memorial of Vikramaditya II.

Fig. 9.19. Right view of the memorial of Vikramaditya II.

Fig. 9.20. Left view of the memorial of Vikramaditya II.

Fig. 9.21. Inside the memorial of Vikramaditya II.

Fig. 9.22. Memorial probably of a queen at Huligemmana Kolla.

Fig. 9.23. Interior view of the queen's memorial.

Fig. 9.24. Nandi in front of a queen's memorial.

Fig. 9.25. Another memorial at Huligemmana Kolla.

Fig. 9.26. Side view of the above.

Fig. 9.27. Temple of Huligemma, known for blessing the devotees who wish for a child.

Fig. 9.28. Inside the temple.

Fig. 9.29. Early Chalukyan carvings on the rock – Saptamatrikas.

PATTADAKAL

Fig. 9.30. Sites opposite the complex at Mahakuta.

Fig. 9.31. Entrance to the temple complex at Mahakuta.

Fig. 9.32. Huchchappayyagudi, Aihole.

Fig. 9.33. Need for proper roads at Aihole.

Fig. 9.34. Huchchappayyana matha, Aihole.

Fig. 9.35. View outside Huchchappayyana matha.

Fig. 9.36. Another view outside Huchchappayyana matha.

Fig. 9.37. View in front of Aihole temple complex.

CONCLUSION

North Karnataka is blessed with such a glorious historical heritage and wonderful landscape and natural beauty that it can be a paradise to every tourist who wants to explore the nature and take a journey into the past.

The onus of making Badami-Aihole-Pattadkal a golden ring is upon the tourist organizations, government, media, academicians and the public at large.

With a few recommendations quoted in my paper, I conclude that we can make best use of the resources and contribute to the state's economy and development.

REFERENCES

1. Rajasekhara, S., *Early Chalukya Art at Aihole*, New Delhi, 1986.
2. www.wikepedia.org
3. asi.net.in

10

Urban Planning of Chalukya Towns

V.M. Hegde

ABOUT TOWN/URBAN PLANNING

- Indicates the arrangement of various components
- Done in such a way that towns as such attain the significance of a living organism
- It includes improvement of existing towns or for the extension of towns
- It requires common sense or understanding of various needs of society occupying or likely to occupy the town
- Town-planning is an art as well as a science
- Needs co-ordination and co-operation of various agencies
- Objective is beauty, convenience and health

WHAT DO TOWN PLANNERS DO?

- Modern profession of town planning mainly arose in response to the urban problems caused by rapid industrialization from the late 19th century
- Needs pioneering professionals from the fields like architecture, surveying, engineering, landscape architecture, social sciences, etc.

- T.P.s could either design new urban areas or develop ways to reform and record existing ones
- Early T.P.s concentrated on securing adequate provision for key urban needs
    - Housing
    - Commercial and industrial uses
    - Water, sewerage and energy supply
    - Open space and recreational area
- T.P. had to be affordable and to fit the designated site
- Vision is produced through a set of drawing
- Planning today—committed to ideal urban environment and planner has to work with challenging political contest
- Much attention is directed towards environmental goals, sustainability, better management, conservation, etc.

ABOUT BADAMI, AIHOLE, MAHAKUTA, PATTADAKAL

BADAMI

- Renowned for affluent history and ancient architecture
- Historic capital of early Chalukya kingdom
- Has splendidly carved monuments and caves of 6th and 7th century belonging to the Chalukyas
- Celebrated for four cave temples
- City came into existence in AD 540
- Caves are famous pilgrim centres of Hinduism, Buddhism and Jainism alike
- The town was also ruled by Hosayalas, Rashtrakutas, Vijayanagar, Adil Shahis Navabs of Savanur, Marathas and Hyder Ali, and later taken over by the British

AIHOLE

- It is one of the oldest places of India
- Ruled by Chalukya dynasty and founded by Pulakeshi I (AD 543)
- Also ruled by Rastrakutas, Muslims, etc.
- First capital of the early Chalukyas, who built over 125 temples in various styles (Fig. 10.2)

Badami, Google map

MAHAKUTA

- Well known as Shaiva centre
- Temples are dated back to 6th or 7th century
- Patronised by kings of the Chalukya dynasty of Badami
- Architecture which is similar to that of temples in nearby Aihole
- Architecture—Indo-Aryan and Dravidan style
- 10 km east of Badami

PATTADAKAL

- Declared as a World Heritage Centre by UNESO in 1987
- Tourist attractions are Sangameswara, Chandrashekhara, Papanatha, Kashivishwesvara
- Second capital of Chalukyan Empire after Badami
- Place became famous because of its variety of temples built in hybrid style resembling the Dravidian architecture, Chalukyan and Nagara style (Fig. 10.1)

Aihole, Google map

FACTS - ISSUES

- Report by GoI Ministry of Tourism (MRD) on Infrastructure gaps in Tourism Sector in Badami – Pattadakal – Aihole, Karnataka

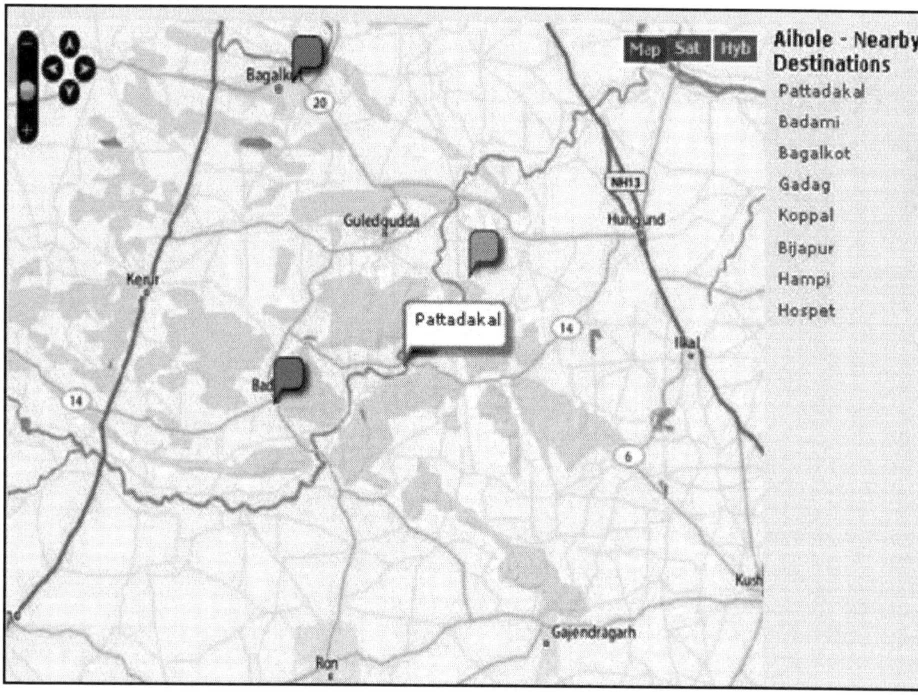

Pattadakal

- Report prepared by GFF MODE PVT. LTD – June, 2010
- Objective of the study—To ascertain infrastructure gaps in Badami – Pattadakal – Aihole – bridge the gap – to increase the volume of tourists

Fig. 10.1. Pottadakal temples.

Fig. 10.2. Durga temple, Aihole.

Fig. 10.3. Badami Google map.

- Study design included interview of tourists (Indian and foreign)
- Foreign Tourists—
  Middle aged (26-55)
  18% younger age (< 25 years), (09% > 55 years)
  1. France and Italy (54%)
  2. USA and Germany (10%)
  3. Other European countries (14.5%)

FACTS - ISSUES

- Stay and visit details
  - 18-25 years of age (44%)
  - 26-35 years of age (31%)
  - > 55 years of age (05%)
  - Karnataka (85%)
  - Maharashtra (08%)

Fig. 10.4. Aihole Google map.

- Tourists

  First time visitors > 76%
  Personal car users > 39%
  Public bus trip split > 36%
  General tourism trip > 83%
  Came with friends> 62%
  > 80% reported they would stay for a day
  > 05% reported through organized trips

FACTS - ISSUES

- Stay details
  - 1/3 - stay at commercial places
  - 1/4 - hired place on rent
  - 21% - staying with friends/relatives

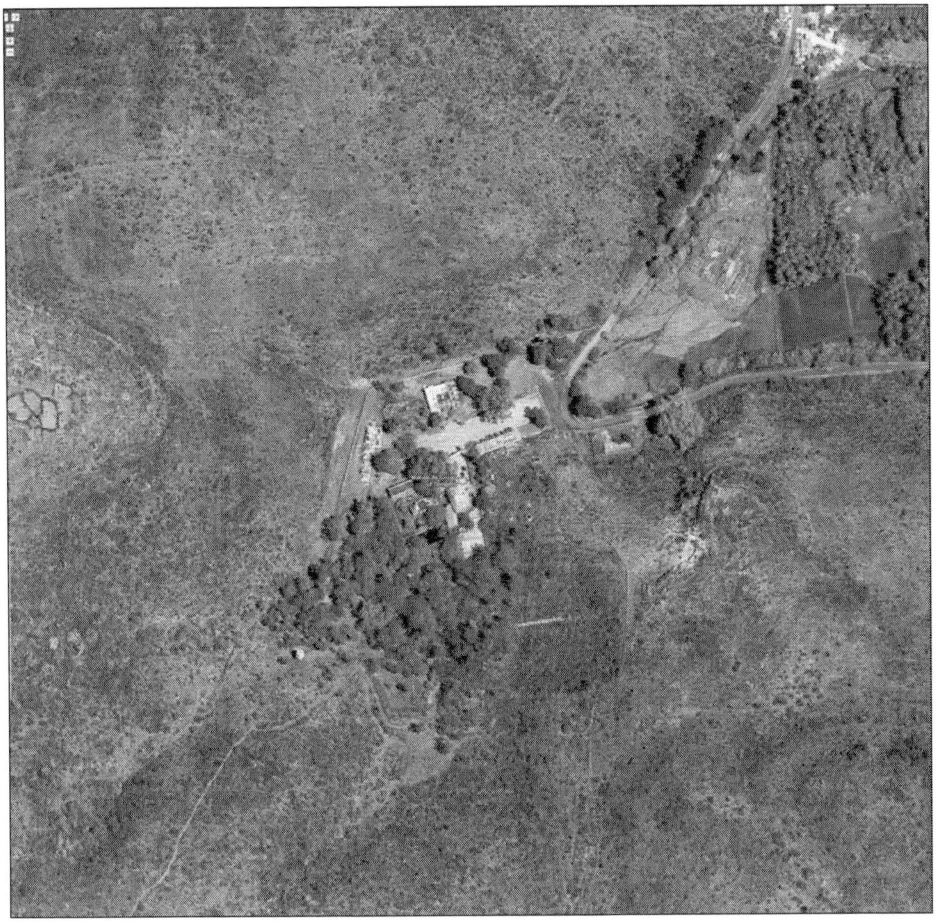

Fig. 10.5. Mahakuta Google map.

- Satisfaction level

Foreign tourists	:	Largest % unsatisfactory Very small % excellent/good Transport 10-20% reported poor
Domestic tourists	:	Connectivity—Average Large percentage—Average satisfaction

Fig. 10.6. Pattadakal Google Map.

FACTS - ISSUES

- Foreign tourists
  - Conditions around sites leave a bad impression about the site. There is a need to improve it.
  - Conditions of signages within the destination need to be improved so that tourist can get enough guidance and information about the site.
  - Infrastructure improvement to approach road is required—conditions of railway station, public conveniences, hygienic conditions of restaurants/dhabas, drinking water, road, telephone is required.
  - Foreign tourists, number is small.

NATIONAL TOURISM POLICY

- Formulated in 2002
- Built arround 7 'S' *mantras*
  - *Swagat* (Welcome)
  - *Soochana* (Information)
  - *Suvidha* (Facilities)
  - *Suraksha* (Security)
  - *Sahyog* (Co-operation)

- *Sanrachnaa* (Infrastructure)
- *Safaai* (Cleanliness)

NATIONAL TOURISM POLICY

- Tourism policy attempts:
  - Tourism as a major engine of economic growth
  - Employment generation, economic development, providing impetus to rural tourism
  - Focus on domestic tourism
  - To tap untapped tourism potential and attract global tourists
  - Enhance the role of private sector
  - Integrated Development of tourism—civilization, heritage, culture
  - Feel Indian from within
  - Incredible India

OTHER ASPECTS LOOKED INTO ARE:

1. World-class standards
2. Infrastructure development
3. Central assistance during different Five Year Plans, e.g. 10th Plan. Fund larger projects—Infrastructure development—in an integrated manner.
4. Destinations are carefully selected
5. Master planning and implementation—to establish backward and forward linkages
6. Funding through state-level consultation
7. Identification of tourism circuits
8. Some components are not eligible, e.g. hotels and restaurants, vehicles and sports facilities

RECENT INITIATIVES—11TH PLAN (2007 – 2012)

1. World-class infrastructure creation
2. Identification of tourist circuits and destinations
3. Karnataka – Projects in Bijapur – Bidar – Gulbarga sanctioned

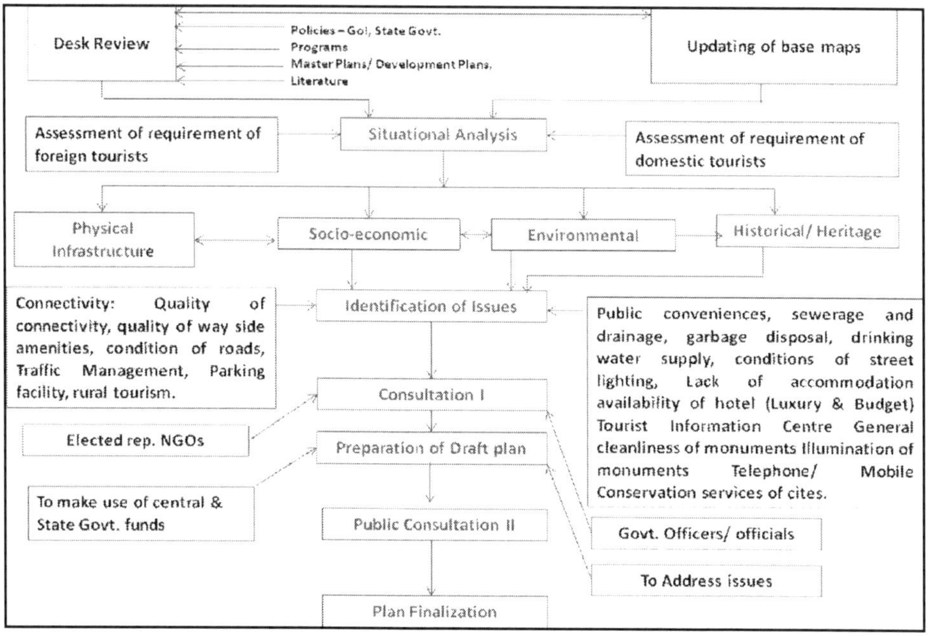

Methodology

Karnataka Tourism Policy—2009-14

1. Earlier Policy—2002 to 2007; Published on 20-01-2003; Atithi Karnataka home stay – wildlife tourism
2. New Policy—2009-2014 for five years
3. Vision—Make tourism Karnataka's principal and largest economic activity, as an employer, revenue generator, and engine of growth, by being among the top tourism destinations in India by 2016-17.
4. Tourism zones have been identified—four zones—Zone 1 to 4

Zone I	-	LPA Bangalore
Zone II	-	BMRDA Limit
Zone III	-	Mysore, Coorg, Hampi, Pattadakal-Badami-Aihole, Bijapur, Bidar, Coastal area from Ilkal to Karwar
Zone IV	-	All other areas

Thrust Areas of Policy are

1. Standardization and classification
2. Culture/Heritage tourism
3. Home stay
4. Bangalore tourism
5. Public accommodation
6. Exhibition complexes
7. Exhibition and convention complexes
8. Theme and entertainment parks
9. Cruise tourism
10. Eco-tourism
11. Health and wellness tourism
12. Adventure tourism
13. Tourism education
14. Safety and security

Investment Proposed

1. Rs. 20,000 cr. investment in next 5 years
2. PPP model
3. 2009 – 14 policy aims to make state one of the largest employment and revenue generators
4. Investment will focus on developing state as a culture and heritage destination and hub to eco-tourism, making state as health and wellness centre.
5. State planning to attract 62 m by 2017 (now 37 million).

11

The Archaeological Museum at Badami

Meena M. Mohite

Badami is situated 40 km south-east of Bagalkot, 132 km south of Bijapur and about 110 km north-west of Dharwad. Badami on Gadag-Sholapur broad gauge is the nearest railway station and Hubli is the neatest airport. A number of buses ply from Dharwad, Hubli, Bagalkot and Gadag connecting Badami.

Badami, the capital of the early Chalukyas, is noted for its cave architecture as well as structural architecture. With the building of an invincible fortress at Badami by the founder of the Chalukya rule Pulakesi I, the capital was beautified by the creation of some magnificent monuments in the form of cave temples and structural edifices. Badami being the capital city for more than two hundred years, naturally attracted the attention of the patrons including the royal family in beautifying the city. Badami along with Aihole, Mahakuta and Pattadakal and other smaller art centres in the vicinity of the above four major centres of art came to be dotted with temples in true Chalukya style. In Badami itself, a few temples are located around the Agasthya Teerth, which is located within the scenic beauty of sandstone formation. This unique place makes an interesting tourist destination.

The Archaeological Museum at Badami, located at the foot of the northern hill, was established in 1979. There was a need for the museum because of the existence of lots of archeological material in the form of inscriptions, hero-stones, loose sculptures, etc. which were lying uncared for around Badami and nearby places. In 1982, the museum was converted into a full-fledged site museum housing pre-historic stone implements, sculptures, architectural elements, inscriptions, old photographs and site model of Sidlaphadi.

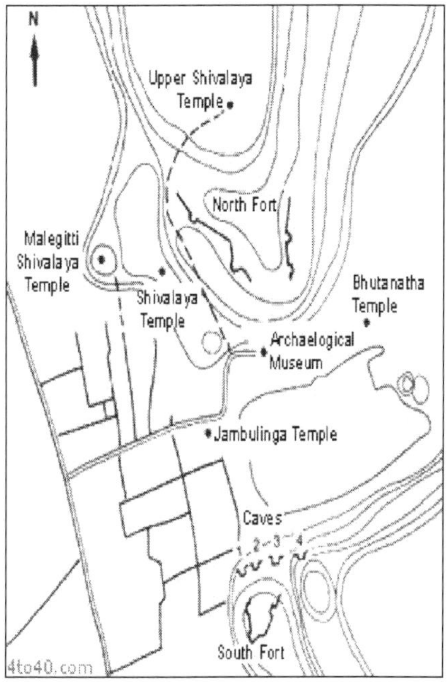

Fig. 11.1. The Site Plan.

The museum building itself is interesting. It is fashioned after the façade of a cave temple decorated with architectural elements like *kudus* and *shalas*. The pillars too resemble the early Chalukya pillars.

In the open air gallery and the open verandah are housed hero-stones of the medieval times and inscriptions in addition to

Fig. 11.2. The entrance gate at Badami.

Fig. 11.3. Open art gallery, Badami.

Fig. 11.4. Lajja Gauri, in Badami Museum.

a few sculptures. A look at the material kept in the museum interests art students. The sculputres of the early Chalukya period add to our knowledge regarding the planning and the execution of the sculpture. Among the objects in the museum, the following deserve our attention. The narrative panel carved in red sandstone is one of the earliest narrative panels to be found in south India. The huge *makara torana*, very articulately chiselled, is a testimony to the artistic creative ability of a later Chalukya sculptor.

However, it is the early Chalukya sculpture of Lajja Gauri that scores over all other objects exhibited in the museum. It may

Fig. 11.5. Badami Museum.

be noted here that the sculptures of Lajja Gauri related to fertility cult are found in a few early Chalukyan sites like Aihole, Naganathana Kolla, Siddana Kolla, Huligemmana Kolla, Mahakuta, Hale Mahakuta Alampur and other places. The Lajja Gauri sculpture in the museum was originally lying by the side of the Naganatha temple at Naganatha Kolla. The sculpture exhibits a female torso. Instead of a head, we have a full but half lotus flower. The legs are bent up and placed on the side in what may be called *uttanapada* posture. This posture is often described as birth-giving posture. That the sculpture is related to fertility cult is beyond doubt. She wears the usual early Chalukya ornaments including the unique *mukta-vaikakshaka*. It may be noted here that she is often referred to Renuka.

Fig. 11.6. Model of prehistoric rock shelter at Shidalphadi.

The museum has a large number of memorial stones erected for different reasons. These include hero-stones, Sati stones, *Penbuyal* memorials, *Gograhana* memorials and *Nisidhi* memorials. Hero-stones (Viragal) were erected to the memory of soldiers, who died while defending/rescuing either the cows or the kingdom or the women who were captured by enemies (*Penbuyal*). *Nisidhis* are of Jains who performed the *sallekhana* rite and gave up their lives.

The museum also houses a large number of early Chalukya sculptures of different deities. In one of the rooms, a model of Shidlaphadi is kept. Sidlephadi is a natural bridge-like cavern with a large hole on the the centre on the top, supposed have been made by lightning. The museum also has wall showcases displaying stone artefacts,

Fig. 11.7. Nandi in the museum premises.

prehistoric art, etc. Outside the museum in the open space are a few sculptures of which that of Nandi deserves our attention.

Outside the museum on a boulder is the well-known Pallava inscription of Narasimhavarman I. After capturing Badami in AD 642 he engraved an inscription boasting of his victory over the Chalukyas and assumed the lofty epithet of *Vatapikonda.*

The museum is closed on Fridays. On other days, it is open from 10.00 a.m. to 5.30 p.m. An entry fee of Rs. 2/- is charged for adults.

Select Bibliography

Annigeri, A.M., *The Cave Temples of Badami*, Dharwar, 1978.

Banerji, R.D., *Bas Reliefs of Badami*, Calcutta, 1929.

Brown, Percy, *Indian Architecture (Buddhist and Hindu Periods)*, 5th Edn., Bombay, 1956.

Burgess, Jas, *Report of the First Seasons Operations in Belgaum and Kaladgi Districts*, London, 1874.

Cousens, Henry, *The Chalukyan Architecture of the Kanarese Districts*, Calcutta, 1926.

Dhaky, M.A., *Encyclopaedia of Indian Temple Architecture, South India, Upper Dravida Desha, Early Phase*, Delhi, 1986.

Dikshit, D.P., *Political History of the Early Chalukyas of Badami*, New Delhi, 1980.

Gupte, R.S., *The Art and Architecture of Aihole*, Bombay, 1962.

Michelle, George, *Early Western Chalukyan Temples*, London, 1975.

Mohite, Meens, *Early Chalukya Art at Mahakuta*, Delhi, 2012.

Nagaraja Rao, M.S. (ed.), *The Chalukyas of Badami (Seminar Papers)*, Bangalore, 1997.

Nilakanta Sastri, K.A., *A History of South India*, 2nd edn., Madras, 1958.

Padigar, Srinivas, V., *Inscriptions of the Chalukyas of Badami*. Bangalore, 2010.

Radcliffe, C., *Early Chalukya Sculpture*, Ph.D. Thesis, New York, 1981.

Rajasekhara, S., *Early Chalukya Art at Aihole*, New Delhi, 1985.
Rajendra Prasad, B., *Chalukya Temples of Andhradesa*, New Delhi, 1983.
Ramesh, K.V., *Chalukyas of Vatapi*, Delhi, 1984.
Saletore, B.A., *Social and Political Life in the Vijayanagar Empire*, Madras, 1934.
——, *Medieval Jainism with Special Reference to the Vijayanagar Empire*, Poona, 1938.
——, *Ancient Indian Political Thought and Institutions*, Bombay, 1963.
Soundara Rajan, K.V., *Early Temple Architecture in Karnataka and Its Ramifications*, Dharwar, 1969.
Srinivasan, K.R., *Temples of South India*, New Delhi, 1971.
Tarr, Gary, *The Architecture of the Early Chalukyas*, Ph.D. Thesis, University of California, Los Angeles, 1969.
Tartakov, G.M., *The Durga Temple at Aihole—A Historiographical Study*, Delhi, 1997.
Yazdani, G. (ed.), *The Early History of the Deccan*, Oxford, 1960.

Index